Risk and Quality Management
in Legal Practice

Related titles by Law Society Publishing:

Becoming a Partner
Young Solicitors' Group
1 85328 841 1

Excellent Client Service
Heather Stewart
1 85328 777 6

Lexcel Practice Excellence Kit (3rd edn)
The Law Society and Web4Law
1 85328 911 6

Managing Cyber-Risks
Rupert Kendrick
1 85328 771 7

New Partner's Guide to Management
Simon Young
1 85328 776 8

Practice Management Handbook
Edited by Peter Scott
1 85328 915 9

Profitability and Law Firm Management (2nd edn)
Andrew Otterburn
1 85328 820 9

Setting up and Managing a Small Practice (2nd edn)
Martin Smith
1 85328 792 X

Titles from Law Society Publishing can be ordered from all good bookshops or direct from our distributors, Marston Book Services (tel. 01235 465656 or email **law.society@marston.co.uk**). For further information or a catalogue, email our editorial and marketing office at **publishing@lawsociety.org.uk**.

Risk and Quality Management in Legal Practice

Matthew Moore and John Verry

The Law Society

ISBN 1 85328 947 7

Published in 2005 by the Law Society
113 Chancery Lane, London WC2A 1PL

Typeset by J&L Composition, Filey, North Yorkshire
Printed by TJ International Ltd, Padstow, Cornwall

Contents

About the authors

Matthew Moore is a director of Web4Law, a law firm management consultancy whose members are the approved trainers in the Lexcel scheme for the Law Society and wrote the third edition of the *Lexcel Office Procedures Manual*, part of the *Lexcel Practice Excellence Kit*, third edition (Law Society, 2004). Matthew advised the committee that produced the 2004 standard and co-wrote the *Lexcel Assessment Guide*, the companion title in the *Kit*. Formerly a solicitor in private practice, he has some 20 years' experience of law firm management consultancy and training.

John Verry is a director of AFP Consulting, a law firm risk and quality consultancy, and a division of Alexander Forbes Risk Services UK Ltd. He has 10 years' legal risk management experience gained working at the Solicitors Indemnity Fund, St Paul Travelers, and as an inhouse risk and compliance officer at a top 50 practice in the City of London. John was formerly a partner in private practice.

Foreword

There is no doubt that the legal landscape has altered dramatically in recent years. To reflect those changes it is important that we focus on establishing a profession that is modern and effective and one that delivers a legal service for 21st century consumers.

With the likelihood of increased competition in the legal market, I believe putting high quality service delivery at the top of the agenda is the only option for firms looking to the future. Those who will thrive are, in my view, those who focus on the needs of their potential client group and who market an excellent service to those clients, be they private or commercial, large or small.

I am pleased to say that more and more firms are now recognising the importance of delivering legal services in a professional, well managed business. I have no doubt that this excellent book will be an invaluable tool to all practitioners and practice managers looking to improve the service that they offer to clients, helping them to explore the link between managing risk and implementing an appropriate quality standard in order to achieve a high quality legal service.

I believe that an accreditation for good quality, such as the Law Society's Lexcel quality standard, provides its recipients with a competitive edge in a demanding market. As President of the Law Society, I therefore commend the Lexcel standard, and this comprehensive publication, to all who strive to meet the highest standards in the service offered to clients. Adopting a quality management approach to legal practice has an enormous value in the modern legal market and I would encourage more firms to choose this path as the route to a better future.

Preface

Law firms of all descriptions and sizes have had to address principles of risk and quality management in recent years. The earlier book by Matthew Moore in the practice management series, *Quality Management for Law Firms*, dealt generally with all elements of a quality management programme – therefore encompassing issues such as business planning, marketing and financial management. *Risk and Quality Management in Legal Practice* confines itself to those elements of a quality management programme that impact directly on operational risk issues – the risk of liability that arises from the firm's day-to-day fee earning activities. Our collaboration means that we have been able to add an insurer's perspective to a consideration of the systems and procedures that form the essential elements of any quality management programme. We hope that the resulting book will be of practical help to practitioners and anyone else who wants to understand the nature of lawyering in the 21st century.

The text contains extensive references to Lexcel 2004 – the quality management standard of the Law Society. It provides a commentary on its key provisions but did not set out to deal with it comprehensively. There is a table of references for those who are working towards an application for recognition under Lexcel or who wish to check that their programme is compliant with its provisions. Where relevant, the Specialist Quality Mark (SQM) of the Legal Services Commission in relation to legal aid work, ISO 9001, and Investors in People have also been referred to, but not in such detail. It is our common belief that the Lexcel standard provides the best agenda for any practice wishing to improve its efficiency of operations through the implementation of a quality standard, whether for the reduction of claims and complaints against it or simply the enhancement of its competitiveness and profitability.

Much in the way of solicitor regulation is in the air at the moment. The book was written before publication of the Clementi Report but its proposals do not directly impact on most of the ground we have covered. The new draft regulations of the Law Society arising from the so-called 'Nally' review are referred to and will probably become effective in much their current format during the shelf-life of this book. Readers will need to keep up to date on developments here if they are important to them.

Matthew Moore: **matt@web4law.biz**
John Verry: **verryj@aforbes.co.uk**

Acknowledgements

Alice Bevington and Maria Kell of Charles Russell Solicitors, for case law research
Sarah Foulkes, Law Society Publishing
Tony Girling, for guidance on costs cases
Stephen Honey, Law Society Publishing
Vicky Ling, for advice on legal aid issues
Rupert Kendrick, for advice on IT liability issues
Robert Mowbray, for the formula on p.60
Andrew Otterburn, for the example on p.106
Tracey Stanley, for her assistance throughout
Giles Watson, Lexcel Manager at the Law Society
Simon Young, for advice on regulatory issues

Abbreviations

ARP	assigned risks pool
CDS	Criminal Defence Service
CLS	Community Legal Service
CML	Council of Mortgage Lenders
CPD	Continuing Professional Development
HMLR	Her Majesty's Land Registry
IIP	Investors in People
LAFQAS	Legal Aid Franchising Quality Assurance Standard
LIB	London Insurance Brokers
LMS	Law Management Section (of the Law Society)
LSC	Legal Services Commission
MHSWR	Management of Health and Safety at Work Regulations 1999
ML Guidance	Money Laundering Guidance (Law Society, at Annex 3B of the Guide)
MLR	Money Laundering Regulations 2003
MLRO	money laundering reporting officer
NCIS	National Criminal Intelligence Service
POCA	Proceeds of Crime Act 2002
SDLT	Stamp Duty Land Tax
SFLA	Solicitors Family Law Association
SIF	Solicitors Indemnity Fund
SQM	Specialist Quality Mark
TECs	training and education councils
TQM	total quality management

References to publications:

The Guide	Law Society, *The Guide to the Professional Conduct of Solicitors 1999*, eighth edition, Law Society Publishing
Lexcel Assessment Guide	Law Society, *Lexcel Assessment Guide*, third edition, Law Society Publishing, 2004
Lexcel Office Procedures Manual	M. Moore (ed.), *Lexcel Office Procedures Manual*, third edition, Law Society Publishing, 2004

Tables of cases, legislation and Lexcel references

Cases

Statutes

Statutory instruments

Lexcel references

Introduction

- New developments
- Why risk and quality management?

New developments

This book is planned as a successor title to Matthew Moore's *Quality Management for Law Firms*. Much has changed since that book was published in 2001. The Solicitors Indemnity Fund was then being phased out and commercial insurers were stepping up their involvement in the indemnity insurance market. Of particular relevance to the insurance industry, the disastrous attacks on the World Trade Center and Washington had not yet occurred. A new version of the Law Society's Lexcel standard was being introduced, which placed much greater emphasis on the areas of client care and risk management. Plans to open up the market for legal services to commercial providers were still a twinkling in the eyes of the Office of Fair Trading and terms such as 'Tesco-law' had not yet been foisted on to a largely reluctant legal profession. Whereas in years gone by the provision of legal services would seldom change to any great degree this was clearly no longer the case.

We now have a very much more mature market for indemnity insurance for law firms. The insurers have learned a good deal about the new market that was presented to them. They were able to build on their experience of top-up insurance (cover above the Law Society minimum requirement of £1 million) and dive into what is somewhat unattractively called the 'dirty end' of the market. The nature of the expectations and demands of insurers, and suggestions on how firms should respond to them, form a major strand to this book.

In 2003 the Lexcel Office initiated a review of the Lexcel scheme and this resulted in a revision of the standard, which took effect from 1 April 2004. This new version of an increasingly popular standard builds on the systems and procedures that had always been required and makes much greater demands on management commitment. Quality management has now to be mainstream to the practice's strategy or non-compliances may arise. Unless otherwise stated, references in this book to Lexcel, with a section number, are to that section of the 2004 standard contained in the Law Society's *Lexcel Assessment Guide*, Law Society Publishing, 2004.

It is, of course, only in recent years that lawyers have had to bother with terms such as quality and risk management. The increasing demands of a consumerist society have put these issues firmly on to the agenda of any practice. Gone are the days when practice management amounted to little more than the senior partner keeping an eye on the bank statements and the partners awaiting with interest the publication of the end of year accounts to discover what sort of distribution they might expect. The modern law firm needs to be an efficient business by any commercial standards. Firms that fail to achieve this risk financial underperformance with the consequential problems of poor morale, inability to recruit and a seemingly irreversible decline in their fortunes.

It would be wrong to represent the interlocking principles of risk and quality management set out in this book as being a panacea. Management devices such as quality standards are tools to be used well or badly. What can be asserted with some confidence, however, is that the firm that commences a thorough programme to review risk and quality is very much more likely to improve its lot in life than the firm that chooses not to do so.

Why risk and quality management?

An important early consideration is why the firm should spend time and money in pursuing a risk or quality project. The sceptics that most firms will count among their numbers will be quick to see the costs and will probably be unconvinced as to any likely gains. The legal psyche seems to need greater proof of cause and effect than other comparable businesses. There may be hard evidence that commercial concerns tend to perform better where a standard such as Investors in People is in place, but that does not mean that the same would be true for a law firm.[1] There may be objective evidence that firms in the Law Management Section (LMS) of the Law Society tend to report higher levels of profit than the norm (LMS annual survey, 2003) but they will say that does not necessarily apply to them. Such arguments are demoralising for the advocates of change and can often be observed to be an increasing tension in partnership management. It may well be, however, that the era of choice on these matters is drawing to a close. Whereas the first firms to apply for Lexcel accreditation did so from a genuine desire to be ahead of the game, most firms now would point to increasing pressure from without. Three main incentives to gain Lexcel accreditation can be identified.

Indemnity insurance

First, and most obviously, the indemnity insurers will expect firms to have taken reasonable steps to reduce the likelihood and amount of claims as a precondition of doing business with them. There is experience of firms gaining an immediate reduction in their premium if they achieve standards such as Lexcel, but it is far from being universal. Every firm should check its individual position with its brokers. There will be those insurers who offer instant rewards (in some cases merely for committing to a programme as by registering on the Lexcel Commitment Scheme) and others who approve but await evidence of real improvements. Broker preferences and claims history are major factors in the range of responses, as we will see in Chapter 3. What seems to be unheard of is the broker who will attempt to dissuade the firm from doing anything to pursue quality standards. A risk or quality programme will always be seen as a good thing, even if the benefits may vary from firm to firm.

Regulation

Another source of increasing pressure is the Law Society as regulator. Emerging from the regulation review is a new draft practice rule requiring practices to be managed effectively.[2] The business operations group within this wide-ranging review process did consider whether Lexcel should be made compulsory but rejected the suggestion. It remains an integral part of the Lexcel scheme that it is a voluntary standard. It forms part of the membership services arm of the Law Society and not regulation. Nonetheless, if a firm wishes to show compliance with the professional regime, what better agenda to work to than a quality management standard devised by the professional body for its members? In the event of a future change of regulator the experience of the banking sector suggests that a statutory regulator such as the Financial Services Authority would be more demanding on such issues and not less. It could be that the choice facing practices is comply voluntarily now or find themselves under some degree of compulsion to do something similar in the future. Experience shows that a voluntary programme is very much easier to manage than one that is imposed and so, understandably, accompanied by resentment within.

Practice excellence

The third source of pressure is arguably the most compelling of all. Practices should institute a programme of risk or quality management because, very simply, it will make them better. If it is the case that firms face increasing competition, they have to improve wherever possible. The more intangible benefits described by firms that have undergone a quality project are linked to morale, involvement and culture. The barriers between advisers and administrative staff seem to reduce – the sense of overall identity increases and the firm becomes a better place to work in. Those interested in improving levels of client care should note that one of the most effective ways to enhance service to clients is to improve morale within. Common sense suggests that a happier workforce will deal more effectively with the public.

Too many practices have perhaps undertaken quality or risk improvement programmes simply to control negative influences that have been identified. There are positive reasons to act as well. Many firms have found that quality accreditation has brought better competitive advantage, especially when pitching for work, and enhanced client and staff retention. Lexcel accredited firms are now given greater prominence on the Law Society website and in Yellow Pages adverts in many parts of the country. Meanwhile work also continues to explain the advantages of Lexcel to other referring agencies such the Citizens' Advice Bureaux.

As to disadvantages, there are firms that would simply associate a programme with an increase in bureaucracy, but these are firms that have not managed the process well. If the verdict on a programme is that quality management simply brings a bigger rulebook with procedures that get in the way of doing the work, the project should be seen to have failed. The aim of the practice should be to achieve greater consistency of standards and processes. The office manual will underpin what it is appropriate to ensure that everyone knows what is expected of them. Wasted time and effort is reduced and greater efficiency achieved.

In conclusion, the reason why any law firm should implement the principles espoused in this book is first and foremost to be a better firm. This should have immediate benefits of increased profitability and will also put the firm into better shape to cope with the wider competition that will emerge from a deregulated market for legal services. For those unwilling or unable to make such a leap of faith the firm's insurers may provide the required inspiration.

One final observation. Should the project be called 'quality', 'risk' or 'client care'? It matters not. The project should be called whatever seems the most appropriate within the firm in question. The net result will be broadly the same whatever the particular priorities that present themselves in any given practice.

Notes

1 A survey conducted by Cranfield School of Management in 1996 found some 'quite dramatic' benefits in IIP organisations – see *People Management*, 6 February 1997, p.30.
2 The new draft Rule 5 imposes duties on principals to 'effect supervision and management arrangements' for a range of issues including the 'effective management of the firm as a whole'.

2

Concepts of quality

KEY POINTS _____

- Business requirements
- Quality assurance and total quality management
- Quality management standards
- Inputs and outputs: revised standards
- Summary

Quality, like beauty, is in the eyes of the beholder. It can be quite a con-tentious term to use in many law firms. Practices that have survived quite happily for decades or even centuries could be excused from thinking that 'quality' is what they have always had to deliver. Clients would have voted with their feet long ago if 'quality' had not been what the firm provided.

Business requirements

The key to understanding the business concept of quality management is to distinguish it from being right on the law. This distinction has inspired a range of different explanations, the most enduring of which is 'real' quality to explain what the firm does and 'perceived' quality to encapsu-late the client's experience. The starting point of a quality management programme is to accept that the two are not one and the same, so far as most clients are concerned. A firm may manage, for example, a difficult conveyancing transaction where there are major problems in the title and planned usage of the property. Resolving these problems takes time and exchange is delayed. In professional terms the advisers have done a job of unimpeachable technical quality, but if their client believes that there was no justification for the delay they may feel that they failed to get their money's-worth. The business view of quality management therefore opens up the prospect of the unreasonably dissatisfied client. In the client's eyes a 'quality' service has not been provided.

This approach to quality brings further unexpected implications. If the above firm had given a competitive quote for the conveyancing work and, notwithstanding the extra work, merely charged its standard fees the transaction would not have been 'quality' work for it. The advice might have been impressive in its technical content but the business view of quality implies a matching of service provided to fees received – a particular problem with legal aid work where increasing numbers of firms have been unable to reconcile the fees received for the work to the level of service and reporting expected by the Legal Services Commission. Common sense suggests that if a firm consistently provides a better service than that which is requested or paid for problems will mount. Over-delivery is therefore just as much a quality problem as the various failures of under-delivery that we might categorise as client care concerns.

Quality assurance and total quality management

It is also helpful to distinguish 'quality assurance' from 'quality management'. The first is a narrower concept that concentrates on whether the goods or services provided do what is expected of them. Quality management is broader and needs to encompass principles of quality assurance alongside other factors needed for the process to succeed. The first moves in quality tended to be assurance rather than management. A problem was recognised in the manufacture of munitions in the Second World War – many bombs were failing to detonate. Traditional methods of improving manufacture, involving testing of the product, clearly were impractical given the nature of the product, so the idea grew that the process leading to the manufacture could be tested instead. This simple concept was refined in later years and consolidated in the international standard of ISO 9001 when it was published in 1979. Quality management is usually associated with the American gurus – W. Edwards Deming most obviously – emerging from work in the post-war years rebuilding Japanese industry. Although often associated with the term 'total quality management' (TQM) this terminology appeared much later in the UK.

Quality assurance is an easier concept to understand than total quality management. The former analyses the process that is key to the business, be it the manufacture of ordnance or the provision of legal advice, and breaks it down into its key components. The analysis leads to a manual of operating procedures – rules that must be followed if the prescription for success is to be met. The process is examined through its life cycle from order or instructions through to conclusion and, in legal terms, archiving. Peripheral elements that impact on the process tend to be included – training in the system and the records needed for later analysis. The main objectives are consistency and reliability of product or service.

Quality management – especially total quality management – can seem more nebulous. It is a management concept that has its factions and there are competing supporters who align with one approach or another, but total quality management produces a challenge to achieve continuous improvement and requires rigorous data collection for measurement and analysis. It is no coincidence that Deming was a statistician by background and many of his methods are regarded as essential elements of quality management by many of its practitioners.

It also should be stressed that quality management was originally developed for industry and engineering. There remain arguments as to whether an essentially industrial concept can be made to work in the professional services sector. The most obvious difference between product and service is that of scientific certainty. Heat a metal bar to a given temperature and its properties and behaviour can be accurately predicted, but provide different employment lawyers with similar instructions and the outcome is much less predictable. Lawyers function in an essentially subjective environment – the reaction of judge or jury, the resilience or flexibility of the other party's representatives – all have a bearing on the client's prospects of success and their assessment of whether they have received a 'quality' service. There are those who claim that on this basis quality assurance does not work with law firms – the preferable view is that it works differently. For many years the Legal Services Commission has experimented with the idea of testing for the 'real' quality of files on audits. Assessments against 'transaction criteria' sought to establish that the right issues had been dealt with but could not actually check the quality of advice provided. Other research has been conducted on testing of predictability of results achieved for clients. As yet there is little to report and the Commission seems to consider that a more subjective 'peer review' may be the way forward. The law is not an objective or a scientific process and outcome will probably always have to be judged by subjective criteria, at least in part.

Quality management standards

Legal aid developments

So how did the law come upon quality management or quality come upon the law? In England and Wales much of the early responsibility lies with the legal aid authorities. In the late 1980s and early 1990s expenditure on legal aid was, to use the much-loved journalistic jargon, 'spiralling out of control'. More money was being spent on helping fewer people and the Legal Aid Board, as it then was, came under pressure to do something to obtain better value for the taxpayer. They turned first to quality assurance. Would ISO 9001 (or BS 5750 as it was then known) provide the solution? An initial thought was that firms providing a legal aid service should be encouraged or required to obtain the standard, but the eventual conclusion was that ISO 9001 would fall short of the mark. Other elements that are key to management – financial controls, people management systems and procedures among them – needed to be part of the requirements. The conclusion was that a management standard needed to be written specifically for the purpose, and Franchising was born. The first version of the standard, which appeared in 1994, drew heavily on the process requirements of ISO 9001 as to how a file should be run, but it also encompassed other elements of management and so could fairly be described as a quality management standard.

Practice Management Standards

The Law Society of England and Wales meanwhile had different concerns that led them into similar territory. A pronounced business recession developed from the end of the 1980s which, unlike former recessions, hit the service sector as hard as it did other sectors of the economy. Many firms emerged from the boom years of the 1980s with greater debt and higher property costs, along with increased partner profit and staff salary expectations. It was an uncomfortable time for most and extremely difficult for some. The Law Society, as the professional body, needed to do something to assist its members. The growth in the profession over the 1980s, especially in the areas of property and commercial work, meant that for the first time many firms had to compete for work. Traditional control of supply and demand had changed and clients now found a buyers' market where they could dictate terms and fee levels. Practice management had come of age and new lessons had to be learned quickly. The eventual outcome was to be the Practice Management Standards. These sought to provide guidance to firms on how they should cope with the increased management challenges that they were now facing. The Standards were approved by the Law Society Council in April 1993 and were commended to the profession as a benchmarking device and as an agenda for the improvements that most firms should be addressing. It was stressed in early publicity that it was not intended to confer external or third party accreditation against the Standards and there was real opposition to this by a number of Council members. It would be another four years until Lexcel would be introduced as a scheme to enable this to occur.

ISO 9001

In common with legal aid franchising, the Practice Management Standards drew heavily upon the process elements of ISO 9001. In the meantime, frustrated by what he saw as a lack of progress, Rodger Pannone – shortly to become President of the Law Society – had commissioned advice on the application of ISO 9001 to his Manchester-based practice Pannone

Blackburn (now Pannone & Partners). The firm underwent a successful audit against ISO 9001 in early 1991 and thus became the first law firm in the world to secure this accreditation. Others followed slowly in the UK and there were international developments as well. Many firms followed suit in Australia, New Zealand and South Africa. The thinking at that time was partly that ISO 9001 imposed purchasing procedures. These in turn would require ISO 9001 organisations to deal only with others that were registered in the manner of some self-perpetuating business virus. Although this was increasingly the case with manufacturing and engineering at that time it never seemed to extend generally to professional services. Gaining recognition under the standard improved the profile of the firm and perhaps advanced them up the list on pitches for work, but failure to have ISO 9001 did not generally prevent law firms from gaining new instructions or clients. There was more pressure in public sector work and certain of the insurers insisted on registration as they started to whittle down their approved panels, but predictions of commercial law firms forced into oblivion by their failure to address ISO 9001 proved to be unfounded.

The early progress of ISO 9001 in the legal sector was not helped by some very poor consultancy advice at that time. The wording of ISO 9001 is alien to those who do not have a background in the sector and unfortunately most advisers insisted on shoehorning law firms into its terminology rather than vice versa. This led to a growing view that the standard could not be adapted to legal practice. To its credit the British Standards Institution collaborated with the Law Society to produce what was described as a 'Code of Quality Management for Law Firms' which was, in effect, a translation of ISO 9001 for the legal market. All of the then 20 sections of the standard were converted into the context of a law firm but this code could only ever be a guidance document and in cases of difficulty the original standard had still to be applied.

As we will see, the later development of all the quality management standards that came into the frame for law firms some 10 years ago has been primarily based on management requirements, especially in the areas of risk and supervision. What is required to manage a file from start to finish has not been substantially revised in any of the standards. It is encouraging to note that the core process of managing the client's instructions has not changed greatly, as yet.

Investors in People

All three of the standards that we have mentioned so far are part of the same family of standards. The Investors in People (IIP) scheme is, and was intended to be, radically different. It is a programme that many law firms have pursued, many in conjunction with one or more of the other legal management standards.

Investors in People emerged from a government paper *Employment for the 1990s* (Cm.540), which was published in 1988. It was critical of the operation of much of British business and of employment practice in particular. Business seemed to be ready to invest in plant and machinery but slow to train its people. New plant was an investment but training was a cost – an attitude still encountered today in many law firms when they work on their annual budgets. There were therefore concerns as to how British business would fare in the single market that eventually took effect in 1992. Such barriers as did exist to protect domestic business were to be removed and the fear was that European competitors were better positioned to succeed at British expense.

To implement the strategy a network of training and education councils (TECs) was established and they assumed responsibility for the new standard that was devised from this initiative. The TECs would be judged in part by the numbers of organisations that they could get to commit to and achieve the standard. Since that time the TECs have been disbanded to be replaced with a range of different business advisory services such as learning and skills councils and small business advisory services. However, government money is still available in certain circumstances to assist organisations in programmes leading to recognition under the IIP standard, thus enabling practices also working towards Lexcel recognition to gain some assistance with that programme.

There were four phases to an IIP programme, starting with a commitment that the organisation would train its people and recognise their role in their future survival and success. Beyond commitment lay planning – the need for a 'written but flexible' business plan and practical steps to involve people in implementing that plan. Action would follow, often with a heavy emphasis on training and then evaluation would show whether the firm had succeeded in its aims (see Figure 2.1).

Where IIP works well it links the overall strategy to all levels of operation within the firm, from departments and teams to individuals. The appraisal process will need to be shaped by strategy and so have some

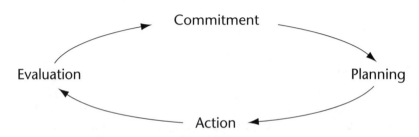

Figure 2.1   Phases in Investors in People

real purpose – personal objectives need to relate to the strategy and any training should be clearly relevant to the achievement of these objectives. To take an example, consider a firm that is implementing a new case management system. The system should be the result of the planning process that will have identified the improvements to client service and profit contribution that should be expected. There is a good deal of attention in the standard to the role of the line manager (head of department or team leader) who will need to be effective in meeting their responsibilities. Everyone might have to review their job description so that any job documentation reflects how people will now actually be working and the appraisals and training will need to examine new skills and how they will be acquired. This linkage is likely to improve both results and morale.

Inputs and outputs: revised standards

Investors in People

It is a feature of all quality standards that they need regular review and Investors in People is no exception. A review of the standard led to the publication of a revised version of the standard in 2000. The most striking feature was a move from inputs to outputs, an important concept in understanding any quality management system (see Figure 2.2).

Figure 2.2   Inputs and outputs

Inputs and outputs can be examined at a number of different levels. At a personal level inputs can be seen as what we do or how we spend our days; outputs are what we achieve. The link between the two is not always as we would wish it to be. There are those days when effort expended seems to bear little resemblance to results achieved. On other 'golden' days everything that we do seems to fall neatly into place and a great deal is achieved.

At an organisational level inputs and outputs are key to all quality systems. Matters that we identified in the arena of people management are set out in Table 2.1 overleaf.

Table 2.1   People management: inputs and outputs

Inputs	Outputs
Job descriptions	Good morale
Induction meetings	High understanding of role and personal contribution expected
Training	
Career appraisals or performance reviews	Skilled workforce
Staff consultation	Satisfactory business results
Supervisory steps – file reviews, etc.	Effective communication, internally and to clients and others
Exit interviews	

Technically, IIP never demanded that certain systems had to exist – there was, for example, no requirement for an appraisal scheme to be in place as such, though it was difficult to see how an organisation could satisfy the IIP description without one.

The 2000 revision of IIP repositioned the standard further away from inputs. In future it would not matter how a firm had met the IIP indicators and the steps that it had taken would no longer form part of the assessment process – all that mattered was that it had achieved what it should have achieved. The various measures in the left-hand column in Table 2.1 were probably necessary but were not essential as such – the matters in the right-hand column were what the standard would seek to assess. There would now be 12 'indicators' of what was expected of an IIP organisation and the 34 accompanying 'evidence' statements would be less important than before.

Problems emerged in assessing without reference to inputs – on later assessments it was difficult to remember what the firm had been doing well three years beforehand. The lack of clear inputs led to difficulties in maintaining standards. In practice, however, the shift away from inputs to outputs was less than expected since hard evidence was still needed to show how the indicators were satisfied.

The 2004 revision of IIP is organised into three phases in place of four, which provide that an investor in people will:

- develop effective strategies in order to improve organisational performance;
- manage and develop its people effectively in order to improve organisational performance;
- understand the impact of its investment in people on organisational performance.

There are now 10 indicators in place of the previous 12 and a total of 39 points of evidence to show how the indicators will be assessed. What very clearly remains within the standard is the emphasis on the planning process converting to specific actions within the firm and then measurement of the improvements achieved. Those who see IIP as being about an increase in training miss the point – the standard continues to harness the contributions that partners and staff will need to make to succeed in any given strategy.

ISO 9001

In common with Investors in People and the Law Society's Lexcel standard, ISO 9001 also underwent a revision in 2000. The process of changing ISO 9001 is very much more cumbersome than revision of the other standards since ISO 9001 is truly international with many thousands of organisations registered to it in most countries across the globe. This inevitably leads to considerable issues of translation and consistency of assessment.

BS EN ISO 9001 (to add the British and European numbering reference) is actually a family of standards. Before the 2000 revision a distinction was drawn between ISO 9001 – the full version of the standard – and ISO 9002, which omitted the 'design' (or matter planning) element. The numbering is now the same whatever the status of the organisation but the design element (or matter planning) now found in section 7 might be excluded where a standardised service such as debt recovery is provided.

There has been sensitivity towards the standard for many years. Quality assurance has often been seen as the poor relation to quality management and ISO 9001 was primarily a quality assurance system. The sensitivity was increased when certain US-based consultants suggested that an organisation consistently producing bad products could still comply. This showed ignorance of one of the most basic tenets of quality assurance in that there has to be a 'quality' system. No auditor doing their job properly could ever consider the production of unsuitable products as being anything to do with a quality system, nor could the product be seen to be meeting customer expectations as the standard has always required. Quality assurance needs a management context, however, and the 2000 revision is described as being a quality management system that links the various related activities that combine to describe the operations of the organisation in question. The standard is stated to promote:

> the adoption of a process approach when developing, implementing and improving the effectiveness of a quality management system, to enhance customer satisfaction by meeting customer requirements.
>
> ISO 9001, 0.2

A further criticism of earlier versions of ISO 9001 was that it merely maintained the status quo and did not place enough emphasis on improvement – a major discrepancy between the standard and the TQM philosophy. A commitment to and systems for continual improvement now form an essential element of the standard. The 2000 revision is worded in terms that are more familiar to the service sector and places a great deal more emphasis on management commitment and planning. It is claimed to be very much more of a quality management standard than its predecessors.

The main provisions of ISO 9001 are now as set out on p.17.

There are those firms that maintain an interest or registration under ISO 9001 precisely because it is a general commercial standard. The argument runs that this standard will mean more to clients since it is one that applies to them as well. The counter-argument is that ISO 9001 is too general a standard and was not written with law firms in mind. We no longer have the legal 'translation' of the standard and it is quite a challenge to apply many of the provisions of ISO 9001 to the operations of a law firm. Who, for example, would associate 'validation of processes for production and service provision' (ISO 9001, 7.5.2) with file reviews, or 'design and development validation' with confirmation of instructions? It is unlikely that an adviser checking counsel's opinion would regard themselves as 'verifying purchased product', and so on. All such difficulties commend the law firm management standards as an alternative and it is not surprising that the numbers of law firms registered to ISO 9001 have declined as Lexcel, in particular, has gained ground. Lexcel retains the useful elements of operational controls that exist within ISO 9001 but in language that any lawyer would understand. As more industries follow suit and develop their specific adaptations of generic standards such as ISO 9001 the status of a standard designed specifically for the profession is likely to grow.

Specialist Quality Mark

When Franchising first appeared in 1994 it was a voluntary code. All assumed that it would eventually become compulsory for those delivering legal aid services and this proved to be the case when the second edition of the Franchising standard appeared in 1998. This version became known as LAFQAS – the Legal Aid Franchising Quality Assurance Standard. This in turn was replaced by the Specialist Quality Mark (SQM) in 2001 with a slight revision to terminology replacing that version in April 2002. There are no current plans to change the standard.

As all involved with legal aid will know, the continual changes to terminology present a challenge in themselves. The Access to Justice Act 1999 introduced the Community Legal Service, or CLS, while criminal work would be the domain of the Criminal Defence Service (CDS). Both parts of the service would be required to comply with the SQM. The

---

BOX 2.1   Summary of main provisions of ISO 9001

---

4. General requirements
    - Identify the processes that are key to the organisations
    - Determine how these processes need to inter-react
    - Examine how these processes can be known to be working
    - Create the right support systems for the process
    - Measure and analyse the operation of the processes
    - Take steps to ensure continual improvement
    - The need for a quality policy and objectives
    - Likewise, a manual and procedures, and
    - Records and reports

5. Management responsibility
    - The need for evidence of commitment by 'top management' to the quality system
    - A quality policy must exist and customer focus needs to be shown, as in client or customer surveys
    - Business planning will need to show 'quality objectives' – measurable targets based on an analysis of the operation of the quality system
    - There needs to be a management representative with responsibility for the system
    - Internal communication must ensure that the effectiveness of the system can be reviewed
    - There also needs to be a regular management review

6. Resource management
    - Sufficient resources need to be allocated to the system and training must also be shown to be adequate to enable people to support the system

7. Product realisation
    - Process controls need to be established and maintained to ensure that the product or service provided meets customer or client expectations and continues to do so
    - There need to be adequate controls on purchasing systems
    - Controls are needed on identification and traceability

8. Measurement, analysis and improvement
    - Customer or client surveys are needed
    - An internal audit programme must be established
    - Steps must be taken when problems arise with the product
    - Data must be reviewed on the operation of the system, and
    - Continual improvement must be an aim, along with
    - Corrective and preventive action when problems arise

creation of the Community Legal Service was an attempt to address the hitherto piecemeal nature of assistance to disadvantaged clients: they might at various times be directed to a citizens' advice bureau, a housing agency and quite possibly a solicitors' firm, but there were no formal links between such outlets. The Community Legal Service would establish local partnerships and committees and liaison would improve. To this end there were three levels of assistance with funding and standards to match:

Level 1   Information Level
Level 2   General Level
Level 3   Specialist Level

Solicitors form level 3 of the service and therefore have to comply with the Specialist Quality Mark. Most refer to this standard as the SQM rather than the fuller 'CLSQM – Specialist Level'. One other change of terminology not really to catch on has been the insistence in the Access to Justice Act 1999 on the uninspiring 'public funding' in place of the time-honoured 'legal aid'.

Although the SQM is a management standard devised for the legal profession it differs from others in two material regards. First, it is enforced on legal aid suppliers who have no choice but to comply unless they wish to drop out of legal aid provision. The second and related point is that the SQM is a 'second party' audit tool – in other words it is used by the Legal Services Commission as a funding agency for its own purposes and the Commission conducts its own audits. This is in contrast to the other standards examined in this book, which are subject to 'third party' audit, in which independent assessors provide a commercial service in checking compliance with the standard in question for use by others. The law firm registered to ISO 9001 can assert to its clients that it has been independently assessed as meeting that standard and that the certification of the assessment body is reliable evidence of that fact. The quality industry operates on the basis that individual suppliers, customers or clients do not therefore need to check for themselves.

The prospect of the SQM being used commercially has always been recognised by the Legal Services Commission (and before it the Legal Aid Board, which they replaced). The introduction to the SQM records that:

> The CLS does not exclude private work. Organisations that are not in receipt of public funding can apply for the SQM and, providing they meet all the quality requirements, will be recognised as full members of the CLS. However, unlike services in receipt of public funds, the audit will not be free of charge.
>
> SQM, April 2002, Summary and Introduction, clause 8

There could be some value in a predominantly legally aided firm paying for an extension to a quality mark audit and asking the auditors to check a conveyancing or other private paying department. The benefit to the firm could be to offer their insurers evidence of an independent audit of the whole firm but it does not appear to have happened in practice, at least to any real degree. From an insurer's perspective it is important that any quality systems are seen to operate firm-wide so the option seems attractive. The nature of the SQM does make it an unlikely standard of choice, however.

There have been varied experiences for firms undergoing legal aid audits over the years. When Franchising was first introduced there were widespread concerns as to the imposition of standards on firms that it represented. There were serious moves to refuse to sign and the Law Society sought advice on whether they hold up the process of firms signing up to the new scheme. Shortly afterward there was an ill-fated 'Birmingham boycott' of firms in the West Midlands refusing to comply with LAFQAS when it was announced. All such initiatives came to nought and the legal aid authorities were able to impose their standard on firms dealing with them. Among many firms is a grudging acceptance that Franchising has improved management standards. The requirements always addressed business plans, financial controls and personnel management systems in addition to case and file records and so had a more general effect than might have been expected, in many cases going beyond the legal aid parts of the practice.

The SQM is organised into the following sections:

Section A   Access to service, including non-discrimination
Section B   Seamless service, including signposting and CLS provisions
Section C   Running the organisation, plans and organisational issues
Section D   People management
Section E   Running the service, including file provisions and file reviews
Section F   Meeting clients' needs, with most of the client care issues
Section G   Commitment to quality, complaints and feedback

Each provision has requirements, definitions and guidance notes. Auditors will concentrate on 'processes' – how things operate in practice, and 'procedures' – a written description of a process.

The experience of most firms with quality mark auditing now is that it is a very much more superficial process than in years gone by. The justification for this from the Legal Services Commission is that firms in most cases have had the necessary systems in place for many years and what once was novel is now embedded in most of their firms. More worrying for legal aid firms in recent years have been the contract compliance audits that arose out of the contracting provisions imposed by the Commission in both civil and criminal work. Limited to just the 'controlled' work arising mostly from initial work for clients (as opposed to 'licensed' work where a full certificate is issued) an audit sample of 20 files is selected to test for non-compliance with the contracting requirements. The scale in relation to this exercise is:

Category 1 0–10 per cent
Category 2 10.1–20 per cent
Category 3 20.1 per cent or above

The implications of the exercise were to be that any firm in category 2 would have to pay the alleged overclaim back to the Commission whereas in category 3 the repayment would extend to all controlled work in that area of work. The view was subsequently taken, however, that since category 2 was also unacceptable to the Commission the clawback would apply to all controlled work in much the same way as for category 3.

The impact of this exercise has been devastating for many firms, especially if they are heavily reliant on legal aid work. An apparently innocuous error by just one fee earner (putting a line through a question on capital rather than entering £nil or £0.00 was a common example) could be enough to place a firm in one of the unacceptable bands with severe financial penalties then imposed. Since the success rate of firms appealing against such findings has been high it seems fair to conclude that the process or the auditing lacked validity and reliability. The current indications are that contract compliance audits will be phased out in favour of peer reviews.

Lexcel

Lexcel – meaning legal excellence – has been in existence since 1997. It remains the process of assessing whether the Practice Management Standards are being complied with. The tendency now is to talk of the Lexcel management standard but in all other respects the scheme has not changed greatly since it was first introduced.

Lexcel is a voluntary standard and is seen by the Law Society as denoting some degree of excellence by the practice. Although it is managed by the Law Society, assessments are conducted independently on its behalf by a number of assessment bodies that otherwise conduct ISO 9001 audits or IIP assessments. Lexcel is an independent management standard but is often combined with one or more of the other standards considered above. The most common combinations are with the SQM for firms with a mixed practice base or IIP. Combining Lexcel with ISO 9001 generally occurs when the firm has had ISO 9001 in place for longer than Lexcel has been available, in which case there may seem to be little point in leaving it to lapse, or because a particular client or funder of work insists on ISO 9001 being adopted, as with some insurance companies.

The original contents of the Practice Management Standards that were the basis for early Lexcel assessments were:

Section A   Management structure
Section B   Services and forward planning
Section C   Financial management
Section D   Managing people
Section E   Office administration
Section F   Case management

These headings survived the first change to the Practice Management Standards in 2000 when new provisions, especially in relation to client care and risk management, were added. Non-compliances at audit have always been classified as minor, which means that the problem is viewed as being capable of being corrected within 21 days and the assessor does not have to return to the practice to see the evidence that it has been put right; or major, if either of these is not the case. A practice cannot be recognised as meeting the Lexcel standard, and so be recommended for the award to the Law Society panel, while there are any non-compliances outstanding. There is now a Lexcel commitment scheme whereby firms can formally declare their intention to work towards recognition and some firms have even succeeded in being recommended for an award on the basis of a pre-assessment – a preliminary assessment for the practice to see where it stands in relation to the requirements of the standard.

Under the chairmanship of John Pickup – the Council member responsible for the scheme from the time of its inception and still in place for the introduction of the 2004 version – all aspects of the standard and its operation were considered. A review of Lexcel with practices in both the private and public sector, along with assessors and consultants, found an encouraging level of support for the standard and general support for making it more challenging. The process initiated by the Law Society in 2003 led to a more fundamental revision than had been expected. The most striking change was the transformation of the standard from six sections to eight, achieved by splitting the long section F in the 2000 version into separate sections on client care, supervision and risk management and then a shorter section than beforehand on case and file management. Section 1, 'Structures and policies' is new and reflects an increased emphasis on management commitment and policies.

The outline of the sections is now:

Section 1   Structures and policies
Section 2   Strategy, the provision of services and marketing
Section 3   Financial management
Section 4   Facilities and IT
Section 5   People management
Section 6   Supervision and operational risk management
Section 7   Client care
Section 8   File and case management

Given that the Lexcel standard is seen as being an excellence standard, and also that the level of management competence continues to rise from year to year in most firms, there was a sense that the level of what is expected from Lexcel had to rise in any event. The most obvious way to achieve this was to look at the issue of inputs and outputs. Lexcel had essentially always been a largely 'input'-based standard with little reason for assessors to question the adequacy of outputs, or results. There was a suggestion that, along the lines of TQM thinking, Lexcel practices should be obliged to set themselves targets that they should be expected to meet. This was rejected on grounds that business performance in private practice will often depend on more fundamental issues than the operation of a quality system. Factors such as the health of the economy, the impact of legal aid funding or the loss of key clients or referrers of work could all render targets unachievable through no fault of the quality system. Similar considerations could apply to employed practices and the many local authority legal departments that have achieved Lexcel recognition. At a lesser level, however, there is more weight given to the quality system actually working and producing the benefits that firms should expect. In the Lexcel standard, outputs now addressed directly on assessment include:

- the ability of the quality manager or representative to have problems resolved (section 1.5);
- the review of the operation of the quality system needing to shape the business strategy of the practice in some way (section 1.6);
- the need for evidence that 'top management' have considered the annual review of health and safety (section 4.2);
- assessors will judge whether recruitment is managed 'effectively' (section 5.3) and whether induction arrangements are 'appropriate' (section 5.6);
- the need for supervision, of both legal work and personnel, to be 'effective' (sections 6.3 and 6.4).

The evidence thus far is that the new version of Lexcel is more challenging but more relevant to practices. There is more room for assessor judgment and this in turn places more responsibility on the assessors to conduct themselves fairly so that some measure of consistency can be maintained in the assessment process. Monitoring the level of assessments understandably continues to be a key function for the Lexcel Office at the Law Society.

Summary

Law firms have a choice of quality standards and all play a part in the management of risk. The legal aid SQM standard and Lexcel are designed specifically for legal practices whereas ISO 9001 and Investors in People apply to any form of organisation. IIP is supported by continuing government subsidy. Legal Services Commission audits of the SQM standard for legal aid firms are as yet 'free' in that they do not give rise to an audit fee, though many legal aid firms would consider that the management time and effort needed to cope with auditing makes the process expensive in practice. ISO 9001 has largely been superseded by Lexcel, which draws from its provisions and benefits from being in legal language as opposed to the 'quality speak' of the international standard. Lexcel is not subsidised as such but can attract funding in some instances when combined with a programme arising from a commitment to IIP.

3

Principles of risk management

Risk is a fact of life and features in all our everyday activities. Risks are just as much present when you are walking downstairs, driving to work or crossing the street as when advising clients later that day. In most areas of our life we may feel that we are exposed to greater degrees of risk than in years gone by – perhaps we are simply more aware of or even obsessed by it. There seems to be a growing consensus that a society that cuts down horse chestnut trees for fear of children falling out of them while collecting conkers is taking risks too seriously. Many who hold this view, however, would also be prepared to sue the landowner in the event of injury. Risk management can be seen in part as a response to heightened levels of claims consciousness throughout society.

It is important to accept at the outset that there is no such thing as a risk-free legal practice. Once we accept that providing a service for clients will always carry a degree of risk what then matters is how that risk is anticipated, recognised and managed. It would be illogical to give up crossing roads for fear of being run over by passing traffic and we learn to take appropriate measures to manage the danger. So too with legal practice – we need to be aware of the risks of claims and liability and manage them accordingly.

What is risk management?

There are numerous definitions of risk management. One of the more common definitions from the financial services sector is that put forward by the Basle Committee on Banking Supervision as:

The risk of direct or indirect loss resulting from inadequate or failed internal processes, people, and systems or from external events.

Basle Accord

The Audit Commission in its guidance on risk management for local government bodies refers to risk management as:

the threat that an event or action will adversely affect an organisation's ability to achieve its objectives and to successfully execute its strategies.

Worth the Risk, Improving Risk Management in Local Government,
Audit Commission, July 2001

The common theme in most of the available definitions is the threat that can adversely affect the achievement of an objective by an organisation. The failure to manage risk properly stands to prevent the organisation from doing its job properly, or at least performing its activities to an acceptable standard.

Risk that is not anticipated and managed is a danger for obvious reasons. It follows that a consideration of risk issues should form part of the business planning process. In many business sectors risk strategies are becoming more detailed and complex. Sometimes risk strategies may be imposed by regulators as a compliance issue but for the most part they are adopted voluntarily. Either way, insurers increasingly insist on evidence of proper risk management planning as a precondition of providing most commercial policies. Beyond compliance, however, a growing number of businesses of all types are coming to see risk management as a management tool that can lead to improved financial performance and which therefore needs to form a major element of core strategy.

Recent years have seen a considerable change in the legal profession's attitude to and its management of risk. Clients have become more sophisticated in their expectations, in terms of the standard of both advice and service. Lawyers are becoming increasingly aware that failure to provide the level of service expected by the client has financial implications in respect of the cost of claims, complaints and loss of instructions. Without doubt, however, the greatest driver of late for the increased uptake of risk management in the legal sector has been the profession's changed insurance arrangements in respect of professional indemnity. It is no coincidence that the profile of risk management in the legal profession increased significantly at the same time as the profession took its professional indemnity insurance arrangements to the open market. In essence the insurance industry provides for the transfer of risk from the insured to the insurer. The insurer is bound to expect that this exercise will be undertaken in a controlled manner – the insured will take adequate steps to manage its own risk exposure as part of the bargain. This in turn means that the insurer's risk exposure will be managed as well. Underwriters will want to know what steps legal firms are taking to manage their risk, and will want proof that they are actually doing what they claim to be

Insurance for the legal profession

Prior to 1975 there was no obligation on solicitors to purchase insurance cover in respect of claims that could arise through their negligence or breach of duty of care. As time went on so pressure to change these arrangements grew. The increasing likelihood of claims meant that deserving claimants might not have been able to gain compensation for losses. The Law Society was understandably concerned as to the reputation of the profession as a whole if such incidents were to become commonplace. Those lawyers who did have insurance had different concerns. Since there was no uniform approach to claims by insurers the perception grew that some insurers were not dealing with meritorious claims as expeditiously as they should have been and were relying on unfair policy wordings to avoid liability. The spiralling costs of insurance were also a growing concern. Largely as a result of the growing claims consciousness of clients the obligation for solicitors to take out appropriate insurance was included in the Solicitors Act 1974. The master policy thereby came into existence.

London Insurance Brokers

In 1975 the Law Society established a specialist firm of brokers – the London Insurance Brokers (LIB) – to manage the master policy scheme. The profession's total insurance requirement was called 'the slip'. The slip was underwritten by a number of insurers up to the cover requirement. Their participation was referred to as 'taking a line' on the slip. One insurer took 'the lead' on the slip, and agreed to underwrite a specific proportion of the cover required. The slip requirement was then arranged by the LIB.

At first all was well and the concerns of the Law Society and the profession that had surfaced previously appeared to have been resolved. The master policy wording provided protection for innocent solicitors from the defalcations of a partner, and repudiation for non-notification of circumstances was protected. Opening premiums were at acceptable levels and the claims handling arrangements were seen to be more in keeping with the standards expected of the legal profession. The principle of 'a fair claim is entitled to a fair settlement' was established. It is in fact possible still to trace some of the facets of the insurance arrangements that apply to today's qualifying insurers back to this original scheme.

Unfortunately, problems grew for the master policy arrangement. As early as 1978 LIB were encountering problems in arranging sufficient cover for the slip. Insurers were refusing to participate and in the early

1980s the situation deteriorated until, in 1984, only one underwriter was apparently prepared to participate. The Law Society had at that time already started to review, once again, the profession's insurance arrangements through the Indemnity Insurance Committee. Various options were considered including the creation of a mutual fund.

Solicitors Indemnity Fund

In 1986 the profession was saved from having to self-insure when underwriters were found who were prepared to take a final line and complete the slip literally at the last minute. It was however clear that the master policy had run its course. After some debate it was decided that the future of the profession's insurance arrangements lay through the creation of a mutual fund, rather than a return to the open market. This scheme – the Solicitors Indemnity Fund (SIF) – was then to survive until 2000 and the return to the open market. Over the 13 years of its operations it would handle some 250,000 reports and pay out in excess of £2.5 billion – disturbing figures however viewed.

The operation of the SIF was governed by the Solicitors' Indemnity Rules. These provisions could be described as the equivalent of the policy wording of a commercial insurance policy. The SIF was obliged to provide cover for all firms and so had to ascertain the potential exposure of the profession as a whole to claims and then collect sufficient money from the profession to meet those potential liabilities. The money was collected annually by way of contributions (the equivalent of premiums) from the profession. There were a number of changes to the SIF's operation during its existence, most notably the increase of the compulsory minimum cover from £500,000 to £1 million and changes to the method of calculation of contributions as the SIF became more sophisticated. These changes steadily brought the scheme more into line with commercial market practices.

Unfortunately for the SIF its existence coincided with one of the most pronounced recessions experienced in this country for many years. The downturn in the economy manifested itself in a number of ways, but most memorably with the collapse in the property market. Repossessions became commonplace and mortgage lenders found themselves incurring huge losses as properties were disposed of for less than the amount owed on the mortgage. The lenders looked to recover their losses and started to review the involvement of the solicitors who had acted on their behalves in securing the loans. It became apparent that in many cases issues as to whether the solicitors had been in breach of their duty of care to the lenders when acting for them did arise. Case decisions went the lenders' way and the SIF started to pay out staggering sums to the lenders by way of damages. This placed the SIF, and thereby the profession at large, under huge financial pressure.

In 1997 it was revealed that there was a shortfall between the amount of the contributions and the potential liabilities (i.e. claim reserves) of the SIF of some £450 million. This liability would have to be met by the profession. It was decided that the shortfall should be cleared over a seven-year period so as to try to spare the profession undue financial hardship. News of this clawback sounded the death knell for the SIF. Pressure grew from those firms with a good claims record and those in low risk areas of practice to be allowed to achieve savings by finding insurance on the open market. Once again it fell to the Law Society to review the profession's insurance arrangements.

It was a difficult decision. The SIF offered:

- a central claims handling function, held by most of the profession in high esteem;
- central collation of all statistical data, including claims;
- 'cradle to grave' cover for solicitors, including 'run-off cover' post retirement;
- control by the profession over its own insurance arrangements;
- no profit expectations from the insurer;
- exemption from insurance premium tax.

Rightly or wrongly the profession believed it was worth sacrificing these benefits so as to have the right to choose its own insurer in the commercial market. The SIF duly went into 'run-off' on 31 August 2000, and after an absence of 25 years the profession returned to whence it originally came – the open market.

Return to the open market: qualifying insurers

To replace the SIF the Law Society decided that a policy wording would be drawn up. To be involved in providing cover for solicitors a commercial insurer would have to agree to abide by certain minimum terms and conditions. If it did so it could become a 'qualifying insurer'. In order to ensure that all sectors of the profession would be offered terms, the Law Society entered into a joint venture with the St Paul International, a US-based insurer. The St Paul, pursuant to the terms of the venture, was obliged to quote for all sectors of the profession from sole practitioner to magic circle firms, but not necessarily all practices.

The Law Society also recognised that some firms would be likely to encounter problems in obtaining terms from the market and, sadly, some would simply overlook the need to do so. It was decided to create an assigned risks pool (ARP) into which such firms would be placed, thus enabling them to continue in practice while they endeavoured to arrange cover from the commercial market. The ARP, it has been observed, is 'not a place to explore out of idle curiosity'.[1] The principal drawbacks are:

1. The premiums are payable on a sliding scale starting at 25 per cent of gross fees.
2. A firm may only remain in the ARP for a maximum of 24 months in any 60 (i.e. two years out of five), and thereafter effectively face closure.
3. Once a firm is in the ARP it is likely to find it extremely difficult to get out and revert to normal arrangements.
4. The damage to a firm's reputation once it is in the ARP, and to the individual partners in it, may be hard to shake off.

In the first year some 31 qualifying insurers were recognised by the Law Society but not all wrote business. The decision to abandon the SIF appeared to be vindicated since the benefits to the profession in terms of cost were immediate. Total premiums payable for the compulsory £1 million of cover dropped from £250 million in the SIF's final year to some £160 million. The great majority of firms experienced substantial reductions in their insurance premiums. Firms at that time perhaps did not realise that they had the Law Society to thank for negotiating the widest cover terms possible in the commercial market. The losses of cradle to grave cover, profession-wide statistics, centralised claim handling, and control over the profession's own insurance seemed to be of little or no consequence to most.

Understanding the insurance market

Hard and soft markets

For many firms insurance represents the third largest overhead after salaries and premises. It is expensive and mandatory and of vital importance to partners in particular. An understanding of how the market operates is therefore useful. One of the most common observations is that the insurance market is cyclical. The cycle is one that revolves around hard and soft markets. Soft markets are when there is plenty of capacity available to provide cover, due to inward investment in the insurance industry. In a soft market an insured may expect competitive premiums and competition for the insured's business. A hard market is created when there is a reduction in financial investment in the industry. Such a market will tend to result in higher premiums, perhaps reduced cover, and generally more onerous terms on the insured. Poorer performing insureds may experience real difficulty in obtaining realistic or affordable terms.

The profession came to the market in a soft cycle and therefore reaped an immediate benefit. The market, sadly, was to change quite dramatically shortly afterwards. Huge claims arising out of the collapse of Enron and the World Trade Center tragedy were blamed, but it was not just these events that were responsible. At the time that solicitors entered the open market underwriters were losing money for the very simple reason that they were not charging enough to cover the risks that they were insuring. Unlikely though it may seem, for every £1 of premium they collected, they were paying out in excess of a £1 in claim payments. Too much reliance was placed on investment income from the premiums to make up the shortfall. Dramatic reductions in the interest rate meant that realistic premiums had to be charged. This resulted in higher premiums. Higher premiums however mean bigger profits and this in turn attracts the investors. In due course more investors will mean more money and this means a soft market – thus completing the insurance cycle.

Calculation of premiums

On average an underwriter will most likely provide for 60p in every £1 of premium to go towards claim payments. Out of the balance business overheads must be met and there will also need to be a profit element to provide a return for investors. It follows that the calculation of the premium is key to a healthy underwriting policy and thus profit. Underwriters arrive at a premium by looking at a number of factors which, in the case of lawyers, will include:

- gross fees;
- work types;
- claims history;
- firm's size and profile;
- burning costs.

Gross fees are a main driver for calculating a premium. The fees that a firm earns usually equate to the volume of work that it does. The greater the fees, the greater the volume of work, which in turn means the greater the risk of a claim.

The work areas that generate the fees are also a factor that an underwriter will look at closely. Some disciplines are regarded as being of greater risk than others. Historically, conveyancing has been viewed as high risk, while criminal law is seen as low risk. Actuaries will calculate the rates that need to be applied to the various work areas so that a premium may be arrived at. The rate is then applied to the gross fees earned in relation to that particular area of work.

EXAMPLE   **Calculation of insurance premiums**

An insurer applies a rating of 20 per cent to fees earned from conveyancing and 5 per cent to criminal fees. If ABC & Co earns £100,000 from conveyancing and £50,000 from criminal law then the premium will be £22,500, made up as to £20,000 for conveyancing and £2,500 in respect of criminal work.

The burning cost of a firm is a useful quick calculator as to how much insurance may cost. It is a simple process focusing on the cost of the claim payments incurred by a firm over a defined period – usually five years. The total cost of claims is divided by the number of years to give an average annual cost.

EXAMPLE   **Burning cost**

Over the past five years ABC & Co has incurred claim payments of £100,000. This makes a burning cost of £20,000 (i.e. £100,000 divided by 5). The underwriter therefore knows that it will have to charge at least £20,000 for an annual premium to meet the costs of the firm's average claim payment.

The burning cost is useful to an insurer but in calculating a premium it will have to add overheads and profit, so the figure is likely to be substantially higher. A common observation made by firms is that although they have not had a claim they are still faced with increasing premiums. It is important to understand that insurance is about cross-subsidies and still, much as in the days of the SIF, the good subsidise the bad. Professional indemnity insurance is no different from any other sector. A car owner may have been driving for 25 years without a claim, but his or her insurance premiums will still have increased to meet the costs of those drivers who do have accidents.

The objective for firms is not necessarily to reduce their premium, but to reduce their rating so as to be able to obtain the best possible premium. A good claims history will always help to achieve this. A good claims history may be achieved through a firm managing its risk exposure effectively in relation to the business operation and the work that the firm does. Many, but not all, insurers will encourage programmes leading to quality awards. All will agree, however, that any practical steps taken to reduce claims will be appropriate steps to take.

Categories of risk

Risk embraces all aspects of the business and the risk identification process must recognise this. There are varying degrees of sophistication with regard to risk categorisation; however, for the purposes of a law firm the following should suffice:

- strategic risks;
- disaster risks;
- financial risks;
- compliance risks;
- operational risks.

Strategic risks

A practice will face numerous business decisions that can impact on its commercial performance. Examples of 'strategic risks' of this nature would include mergers and changes to office locations. In the legal profession the most public problems have arisen in unsuccessful mergers where the parties have subsequently concluded that they were incompatible, with a demerger following shortly thereafter. Financial performance is obviously affected by problems that arise under this heading.

Disaster risks

Few firms have made any provision for business interruption or disaster recovery. Good corporate governance dictates that any business organisation has in place effective contingency plans to enable the business to continue trading in the event of an interruption to its business. The total destruction of the firm's premises may be highly unlikely but situations where the firm is unable to trade from its business premises by reason of a temporary problem should be seen as distinct possibilities. Firms have experienced such problems following a gas leak, power failure or a fire in adjoining premises. Whatever the problem, the firm must be in a position to continue to practise with minimal interference to the client's work. This may mean recourse to alternative premises or accessing offsite backup IT facilities. People will need to know where they should go and what they should do in the event of such a problem. All of this should be addressed in the firm's business interruption plan, which should be both reviewed regularly and also tested to see if it actually works (see Chapter 4, 'Business continuity').

Financial risks

The financial impact on the firm of certain risk events should be kept under regular review. In some firms there may be an over-reliance on fee income from either one client or a particular team. What happens if that client is lost to a competitor or the team is lured away to another firm? It is important, so far as possible, to spread financial risks across the firm so as to lessen the impact of a single event on the firm's financial viability. There will also need to be systems and procedures in place to manage potential theft or fraud within the firm. These may include procedures to monitor cheque signing and access to the firm's banking. Likewise, bad debts, levels of work in progress and unbilled time are all potential risks that need to be managed.

Compliance risks

The profession is not comfortable with many compliance issues. This fact is underlined by the high levels of non-compliance with statutory and regulatory obligations. Compliance considerations include money laundering, data protection, health and safety issues and professional conduct rules. The growing volume of regulations on diversity in employment forms an important strand under this heading. Non-compliance can have serious consequences for firms and individuals. The penalties can be civil, professional or, increasingly, criminal.

There is interaction between the various risk categories and some areas of risk may arise in more than one category. For example, health and safety may be viewed as a compliance risk and also an operational risk, i.e. non-compliance with a health and safety risk may result in the office being closed down. It is important, however, to attempt to keep risk management as simple as possible. The more complex the processes, the more difficult compliance becomes. The important factor is that lawyers understand the categories of risk that they face, that risk embraces all areas of business, and that all members of the firm must therefore comply with the internal processes and procedures.

Operational risks

Perhaps the most obvious category of risk is that relating to carrying out the day-to-day fee earning work of a law firm and the consequential risks of claims, complaints and reputational damage. Although all risk areas have to be accorded due attention it is operational risk that is the main consideration in terms of frequency and severity of claims. It is in this area that the underwriter will expect the insured to be able to demonstrate an understanding of the risks facing the firm, and also to demonstrate the ability to manage the risks. This will most likely be achieved through the use of processes and systems of the type envisaged by Lexcel. It is the failure of those systems and internal processes, as envisaged by the Basle Committee on Banking definition of risk management, that will lead to claims and losses. As each year of the open market passes the underwriters are becoming more aware of these operational risks and have developed a greater understanding of them. The underwriters' expectations have also grown in sophistication.

Common claims

The area of operational risk deserves closer examination in view of its importance within the context of managing risk within a law firm. Unfortunately, as already stated, central statistics relating to claims have not been compiled since the SIF ran down its operations. This is regrettable in terms of effective risk management since this data would identify existing, new and emerging trends in claims. Statistical data is still published, but it tends to relate to each particular insurer or broker and is not therefore so authoritative. An insurer whose book consists mainly of litigation firms, for example, might say that missed time limits are a problem, whereas an insurer whose book consists mainly of non-contentious work might see few problems from missed dates. Although an up-to-date view of the profession's performance is difficult to obtain, the SIF did undertake considerable analysis of claims data during its existence and there is little reason to believe that there has been any material change in the few years since. The Risk Management Unit established by the SIF in 1996 amounted to an attempt to help the profession understand the risks it faced and how to manage those risks. The Unit produced a considerable amount of advice on the common mistakes made in the various disciplines and also what it termed the underlying causes of claim. These underlying causes were the common themes that were identified as being present in nearly all claims, irrespective of the area of law involved. The common pitfalls were what went wrong and the underlying causes identified how these mistakes happened.

Research by the Unit supported the view that the underlying causes of claims tended to arise out of service delivery failure on the part of the solicitor rather than technical legal errors. The Unit's conclusion was that it is not so much a matter of getting the legal advice wrong as suffering administrative failures that resulted in a defective service. The principal culprits emerged as:

- failure to manage critical dates and time limits;
- failure to progress matters and review files;
- failure to communicate effectively;
- failure to supervise and manage work and staff processes;

- failure of internal processes and systems;
- failure to keep up to date with law and legal and compliance obligations.

Failure to manage critical dates and time limits

Historically, the most common cause of claims against solicitors results from missed dates of various descriptions. While the risk is greater in some areas of work than others, every file is likely to have at least one time limit on it. This date might be statutory, regulatory, contractual, or simply a timescale agreed with a client or third party. The problem of missed time limits was recognised by the SIF, which introduced the penalty deductible in respect of those claims that arose out of missing certain identified time limits. In such circumstances the firm had to pay twice its normal 'deductible' – that part of the claim payable by the firm before the SIF made any claim payment.

Many claims for missed dates and time limits remain startling in their simplicity.

> EXAMPLE   **Landlord and Tenant Act 1954 claim**
>
> Firm A, well experienced in matters under the Landlord and Tenant Act 1954 was instructed on behalf of a tenant in the renewal of the tenant's lease. The solicitor acting had in excess of 20 years' experience in such matters, yet failed to serve a counter-notice within the prescribed time limit and the tenant lost the right to renew. The landlord wanted the premises back as it intended to redevelop the site. A substantial claim followed. The solicitor was unable to explain why he had failed to take the appropriate action other than to say he had 'overlooked the date'.

One of the most common problems under this heading is the continuing failure by conveyancers to register their applications at the Land Registry within the priority period afforded by their search. Although in the great majority of matters this will not result in a claim, this will be through luck as opposed to good judgment. There are bound to be concerns about the apparent unprofessional approach and lack of care for the client's interests in firms where this is common practice. Nor are such problems merely the preserve of domestic property lawyers.

> EXAMPLE   **Failure to register option**
>
> Firm B was instructed by the tenant in connection with the grant of a lease of commercial premises. There was an option to purchase the freehold at a

fixed price, which could only be exercised if the option was registered as a land charge or at HM Land registry within 28 days of completion of the lease. This was not done. The business was a great success and the tenant decided to exercise the option to purchase the freehold so as to be able to borrow funds from the bank, who were only prepared to lend against the security of a freehold interest. The tenant was unable to exercise the option. The landlord did sell, but a price considerably in excess of the fixed price set out in the lease. The solicitor's insurers had to make up the difference.

Failure to progress matters

This is a common cause not only of claims, but of complaints as well. The perception that lawyers take too long to deal with matters is widely held. Although misplaced in many cases, it is correct in others. The failure to be proactive on files leads to a dissatisfied client, which in turn leads to complaints and often claims. It is crucial that files are managed effectively and that the client's expectations are addressed. Where the client has unreasonable expectations, the issue needs to be discussed.

EXAMPLE   **Expiry of limitation period**

Instructions were received by a firm in relation to a tripping accident. Relatively minor injuries were sustained by the client, or so it was thought. Little happened on the file for some two years. By the firm's own admission, the fee earner had failed to 'get to grips with the file'. When there was one week left before limitation expired the urgency of the matter was recognised, especially when it became apparent that crucial documents needed to issue proceedings were either missing, or had not been obtained. In the ensuing rush to issue and serve the proceedings it was not noticed that the proceedings had been issued against the wrong defendant. By the time this came to light the limitation period had expired. The client was the wife of a very important commercial client of the firm who subsequently withdrew all instructions, which had a considerably adverse financial impact on the firm.

EXAMPLE   **Failure to preserve value of portfolio**

In another matter an estate consisted of a substantial share portfolio, and little else. Instructions were received to sell the portfolio but the file was put to one side and a delay occurred as more urgent matters were dealt with. Some three months later the stock market collapsed, and over 60 per cent of the £400,000 share portfolio was lost, virtually overnight. Predictably, difficult issues as to the delay experienced arose.

Delay in dealing with instructions to draft a will has resulted in numerous claims against solicitors. The case of *White* v. *Jones* [1995] 2 AC 207 established the principle that a solicitor owed a duty of care to those who might have inherited under an estate and this opened the floodgates for this particular type of claim. Notwithstanding the many subsequent decisions on this point, many solicitors still fail to draft the will in a timely manner, thereby opening the possibility of claims from disappointed non-beneficiaries.

Failure to communicate

Lawyers have to be effective communicators. It is an essential element of the solicitor–client relationship that the lawyer obtains all the relevant information from the client so that the appropriateness of any action taken can be judged.

EXAMPLE   **Failure to establish intended use of property**

Instructions were received by the firm to act in connection with the purchase of a large residential property. While the lawyer acting established what the clients were buying, he did not ask why they were buying it. It was in fact their intention to convert the premises into a residential care home. They were unable to do so because of planning and licensing problems. The clients made a claim against their lawyers saying that they had failed to establish the intended use of the property, which if they had done so would have enabled them to identify and advise the client of the potential problems.

Another example of failing to communicate effectively arises out of the lawyer's failure adequately to advise on the merits of the case and likely prospects of success.

EXAMPLE   **Failure to advise on the merits**

The client instructed the firm in relation to a boundary dispute. Three years later with a bill for £40,000 costs, together with an order to pay the other side's costs, and the boundary still in the same place the clients were very unhappy. The judge had described the evidence as being crystal clear as to where the boundary lay. The clients stated that if their lawyer had advised properly in relation to the evidence available then they would not have proceeded.[2]

Often the adviser may claim that such issues have been discussed early in the matter but it is essential that a record should be made in writing of any advice given or instructions received.

EXAMPLE   **Failure to record advice given**

A conveyancing lawyer acted for an unmarried couple in the purchase of their property. The couple subsequently parted and it transpired that the property was held as joint tenants, notwithstanding that the one party had put in all of the equity. As a result of this the other party received one-half of the equity. The principal contributor sued the lawyer who had originally acted, alleging that he had not been advised as to the meaning of joint tenants and tenants in common and the implications. The lawyer claimed definitely to have advised the clients as he always did. There was, however, no letter or attendance note on the file confirming that the point had been addressed. The claim succeeded.

Failure to supervise and manage work and staff processes

The topics of delegation and supervision are dealt with in their own right elsewhere in this book (see Chapter 5). A couple of examples here might assist to illustrate the importance of the topics.

EXAMPLE   **Lack of experience**

A partner in a firm had a complex probate administration to deal with and had fallen out with the executors who were unhappy with the delay. The file was passed on to a newly qualified solicitor with little probate experience. In order to please the executors the junior lawyer rushed to complete the administration and distribute the estate. Unfortunately the lawyer believed that the inheritance tax liability had been paid but it had not. The partner was 'too busy' to see the fee earner. The beneficiaries were not prepared to return their cheques which they had been waiting for. The tax had to be paid by the firm and considerable time was spent trying to resolve the situation with extremely irate beneficiaries and executors.

EXAMPLE   **Overwork**

In another firm there was a young lawyer who was always keen to help. This resulted in a number of fee earners delegating files to him. There was no record of which files were delegated and to whom. Unfortunately the lawyer was reluctant to seek help on files as he did not wish to be seen as a nuisance. As a result he got hopelessly out of his depth, and came under severe pressure from clients. He began to lie to clients as to the true position in their matters, then proceeded to forge court documents to support his lies. He then made up settlements that he had allegedly obtained for clients from insurance companies, and stole client money to make the payments. The extent of the problem only became apparent when the accounting irregularities came to light some while later. There were 14 files where little or no progress had been made and all became subjects of claims.

Failure of internal processes and systems

Where firms go to the time and expense of creating systems to manage their risk exposure it is important that they monitor compliance. Failure to do so may well mean that the time and trouble involved in establishing the systems was wasted – worse still, the firm may have been lulled into a false sense of security. Perhaps one of the most common examples of this is post checking. Many firms have a procedure for signing post but it often tends to be honoured in the breach rather than the observance. Where the partners have no intention of checking outgoing post this should be recognised. Agreeing on a procedure that few in the firm will follow serves nobody well. Classic examples of claims arising from failure to supervise post have included post going to the wrong address, letters not saying what they are meant to say, and incorrect enclosures.

EXAMPLE   **Post sent to wrong parties**

In a commercial property purchase the client was buying a development plot, and selling it straight on to a sub-purchaser at a good profit in a 'back-to-back transaction'. Unfortunately the lawyer's secretary sent the contracts to the wrong parties with the result that the sub-purchaser received a copy of the contract between the seller and the purchaser. The sub-purchaser contacted the seller direct with a significant loss to the main purchaser, who duly made a claim.

Failure to keep up to date with law and legal and compliance obligations

Although legal errors may represent a surprisingly low proportion of claims against firms they do feature nonetheless and the importance of being right on the law should never be overlooked. Often problems stem from the firm failing to recognise its limitations of expertise. A particular problem area has been firms acting for clients in connection with matters in a foreign jurisdiction – Spanish conveyancing being an unfortunately common example. Where the firm or the adviser lack expertise the matter should not be taken on, however straightforward it may seem. Having purchased a timeshare for oneself should not be seen in itself to be sufficient qualification to act in property transactions in foreign jurisdictions.

> **EXAMPLE** Advice given in matter outside lawyer's expertise
>
> Instructions were given to a lawyer to act in a complex commercial property transaction. The lawyer struggled with the complexities and eventually managed to complete the matter. Unfortunately he failed to realise that the transaction had given rise to a taxable event in the sum of approximately £100,000.
>
> In another matter a commercial client was chatting with his lawyer during a break in a long drawn-out completion meeting. He said his wife had had a traffic accident and suffered a badly broken leg. The accident, he volunteered, had happened nearly three years ago. The lawyer volunteered the information that she ought to do something fairly quickly as he thought that the limitation period was four years. In the claim that followed the commercial client alleged that he and his wife had relied on what the lawyer had said, and lost the right to pursue a claim. The lawyer said that it was an informal discussion and nothing more.

The nature of most claims made against solicitors seems not to have changed greatly in recent years and it is perhaps rather depressing to observe that lawyers seem to make much the same mistakes now as they did 10 years ago. This should also encourage firms to address the area, however, since they can be confident as to the problems that need to be addressed. The topics covered in the following chapters should form the basis for the policy and procedures required. Where commitment can be given to a programme it will make a difference.

Notes

1   Comment attributed to Tony Girling in one of his lectures on the topic.
2   On the professional obligation to consider the cost-effectiveness of the action recommended, see the Solicitors' Costs Information and Client Care Code, para.4(k).

4

Management policies

- Why management policies are required
- Quality policy
- Discrimination
- Health and safety
- Data protection and computer use
- Business continuity

Why management policies are required

Organisations of all descriptions are required to have an increasing number of policies in place. Failure to adopt the necessary devices can lead to civil, criminal and professional liability. The first section of Lexcel is headed 'Structures and policies' and aims to cover most of the policies that are important to practices – the one exception being the requirement for a client care policy at section 7.1. The more general wording of policy statements has in most cases to be supplemented with detailed plans or procedures and these are detailed in different places within the standard.

All too often policies are the right words in the right place with little real commitment to bring them to life. Within Lexcel some attempt has been made to address this. A policy is defined in the accompanying guidance as:

> a general approach taken within the practice to the issue in question. A policy defines why a particular approach is adopted by the practice. Since it is only a general approach there may be stated exceptions from it, but it would be assumed that the policy will apply unless otherwise stated.

The implication of this wording is that if an assessor feels that what has been observed in the practice does not bear sufficient resemblance to the stated policy it could be reported as a non-compliance. For this to be the case it is envisaged that there would have to be some evidence of systematic deviation from the policy as opposed to isolated failures to meet the aspired level.

Areas such as business planning and information technology require 'plans' under Lexcel. These are defined in the guidance as:

> an outline of where a practice desires to be in the future and describes how it intends to arrive at that destination. A plan can be described as a map which supports practices to arrive at their desired destination in the future.

A plan does not necessarily need to be in writing but the wording of section 2 of the standard on business planning and marketing makes it clear that some form of documentation will be required under its provisions.

Quality policy

Requirement for a policy

There are requirements in Lexcel for a 'risk management strategy' to be in place under section 1.3 and a 'written quality policy' under section 1.4. The two elements could be combined, perhaps with the client care policy required by section 7.1. Where responsibility for risk and quality is shared it may well be that the person described in section 1.5 as the designated quality representative is also the risk manager. Where responsibilities are split, the issue of who reports to whom should be set out somewhere. The ability of the quality representative to deal with problems is dealt with in the standard – section 1.5 requires that the 'designated individual who has particular responsibility for the quality system' must have 'sufficient authority and seniority to raise concerns regarding the quality system and to have any such issues resolved'. This provision might come under scrutiny if a problem emerges and is not dealt with by the time of the next annual maintenance visit. Could this suggest that the firm's arrangements for managing quality are not robust enough to ensure that problems are actually being dealt with?

The quality policy required by section 1.4 is described as being:

> a high level document setting out the organisation's commitment to quality and overall policy. Practices will also have documented procedures as set out in this standard, which will be distributed and published throughout the practice showing:
>
> a: The role that the quality system plays in the overall strategy of the practice.
> b: Who has responsibility for the management of the quality system.

The wording requires a linkage between the quality policy and the main strategy of the firm. The quality system can all too easily become a stand-alone element of management with a sense that it is marginalised from the things that really matter to the partners – usually financial. The Lexcel standard expects the partners to see their quality system as a driver of performance and for this view of the system to be apparent throughout the firm.

Reviewing the policy

Section 1.6 of Lexcel introduces an expectation of continual improvement. In addition to the review of the operation of the quality system 'at least annually' there has to be a process for people within the practice to be able to suggest improvements to the system. Again, the intention is to make quality mainstream to the strategy of the practice by requiring the review to 'show the part that the quality system is intended to play in the future strategy of the practice over the next 12 months at least'. The most appropriate method of showing the role of the review of the quality system in future strategy is to include some objectives shaped by the review. These could be as diverse as the elimination of a certain error leading to notifications to the insurer or the conduct of internal training for all personnel on risk improvements. What is important is that the system is not seen merely to detect problems – something has to be put into place to do something about them.

It is not just Lexcel that makes such connections. In ISO 9001 there is a requirement that:

> Top management shall provide evidence of its commitment to the development and implementation of the quality management system and continually improving its effectiveness . . .
>
> ISO 9001, 5.1

The same provision goes on to list such issues as internal communication and the conduct of management reviews. There is a similar requirement for a management representative who 'irrespective of other responsibilities' has the task of ensuring that suitable processes are in place and being improved where possible (ISO 9001, 5.5.2). In Investors in People, with its slant on organisations improving through the contribution of personnel within the firm, there is an evidence statement under the strategic requirements that 'managers can describe how they ensure that people are involved in translating organisational aims and objectives into team and individual objectives' (IIP, 1.3).

As suggested above, many firms working to the Lexcel standard will choose to combine the quality policy with the client care policy required at section 7.1. There will be little difference in practice between the need for a quality policy and 'a documented policy for client care' that includes the 'practice's commitment to provide services to clients in an appropriate manner'. Reflecting the more technical elements of client care in legal practice, section 7.1 also requires the client care policy to set out the procedures for complying with the professional rules of conduct.

Discrimination

Requirement for a policy

Discrimination in relation to the provision of services and the employment of personnel is prohibited by both the general law and the professional rules. Legal aid firms also need to take heed of the SQM, which makes separate but similar requirements in relation to those who provide publicly funded services (SQM 2002, section A3 in relation to the provision of services and section D1.3 on the 'selection, treatment and behaviour of staff').

The Law Society's rules were overhauled in October 2004 when the previous Anti-Discrimination Rule was replaced by the Solicitors' Anti-Discrimination Rules 2004. As before, the professional rules go further than the law of the land. Solicitors could therefore find themselves liable for professional misconduct even though they have not breached any legal requirements, as the guidance that accompanies the Anti-Discrimination Rules 2004 makes clear. The guidance also states that there will be further legislative developments in this field, which solicitors should monitor.

Race, sex and religious discrimination

So far as the legal position is concerned, the combined effect of legislation such as the Race Relations Act 1976 and the Sex Discrimination Act 1975 is that it is unlawful to discriminate against individuals on stated grounds either directly or indirectly whether in regard to the provision of services or employment opportunities. The law also extends to the outside instruction of others such as counsel (Race Relations Act 1976, s.26A(3) and Sex Discrimination Act 1975, s.35A). The professional rules date from 1995 when the Solicitors' Anti-Discrimination Rule was first brought into effect. At first, discrimination against creed and religion was not included in the Rule although it did appear in the legal aid provisions (guidance to SQM 2002 at p.37 – section D1 'Model policies'), but it has since been added. The inclusion of sexual orientation within the Rule has not been without controversy and has been opposed by practitioners with certain religious views. Likewise, there have been difficulties where a firm has an ethos that is shaped by a particular religion and the preference is to recruit fellow believers.

Firms are required to adopt a policy dealing with the avoidance of the listed areas. There is a Law Society model policy, which does not have to be adopted as such, but where firms choose to draft their own documentation it must cover all of the matters referred to in the model policy and to the extent that firms fail to do so it is implied that they have adopted any provisions that are omitted.

A schedule to the Law Society's earlier model policy introduced targets for greater ethnic balance in the employment profile of job applicants, the stated aim being to 'give ethnic minority trainee and qualified solicitors as fair a chance of employment as their white counterparts'. These were stated to be targets for good practice rather than enforceable quota and suggested at least one fee earner from an ethnic minority in small firms (6–10 fee earners) and at least 10 per cent of their trainees and 5 per cent of other fee earners of ethnic minority in larger firms. It was heartening to read of progress in this area in the annual statistical survey of 2004 as reported in the *Gazette*:

> The proportion of practising solicitors from ethnic minorities has risen to match that of the national population, figures this week have shown. According to the Law Society's annual statistical report the percentage of practising solicitors in England and Wales from ethnic minorities increased from 7% to 7.9% last year. This is the same as the Office of National Statistics figure for the UK population as a whole.
>
> [2004] *Gazette*, 8 July, 3

Whatever the general picture, the risks to any given firm through not applying the model policy in line with good practice quite clearly remain. Many firms remain exposed to allegations of unfair practice and thus potentially damaging and costly claims. An occasional review of management practice is advisable to ensure that procedures throughout the practice continue to support the required policy.

In most firms the recruitment and promotion of personnel probably represents the area of greatest vulnerability in relation to discrimination and unfair practice. The problem is less likely now to be blunt discrimination intended as such, so much as employment practices that are unlikely to provide fair opportunities for all. The principal recommendation from most of the advice available from the various agencies is that recruitment should always be an 'open' process – in other words, all positions should be advertised. Failure to do so – most commonly by recruiting through word of mouth – is likely to perpetuate any current imbalance in the workforce. An open recruitment process is a requirement of the SQM for legal aid firms and should be seen as important elsewhere. Application forms are recommended since they tend to encourage greater fairness in comparisons that are made between different applicants. Finally, the same questions should be addressed to all candidates in interviews and notes taken and maintained for 12 months. It is becoming standard personnel practice to provide feedback to unsuccessful candidates and provisions to this effect can be found in Lexcel at section 5.3f and the SQM at section D1.4 as part of their respective requirements for an open recruitment process.

Disability discrimination

The prohibition of discrimination against disabled people is more recent in its statutory origin and may need greater attention as a result. Law firms are 'service providers' under the Disability Discrimination Act 1995 and thus owe duties to clients, applicants and employees. The Act makes it illegal to discriminate against a disabled person by refusing to provide them with services or by providing services to a different standard or on different terms. Discrimination is deemed to have occurred where the firm fails to make 'reasonable adjustments', most obviously in relation to the design and use of premises. This duty does not arise only when it becomes an issue, since the duty is owed to disabled people in general. Problems should therefore be anticipated and planned for in advance. The test of reasonableness in failing to make adjustments is based on whether others would think that the time, inconvenience, effort, discomfort or loss of dignity involved in using the service would be considered unreasonable by others if they had to endure similar treatment.

The working environment

Increasingly, issues of discrimination are issues for the partnership itself. It is worth emphasising that the Law Society's model anti-discrimination policy extends equally to partners and staff. Discrimination may arise from the nature of the working environment, as where many of the marketing activities appeal particularly to men, and where success in marketing is seen as one of the criteria for promotion to membership of the firm. Working hours and patterns are also a concern in this regard and formed a central feature of *Sinclair Roche & Temperley* v. *Heard* [2004] IRLR 763, where two female salaried partners claimed that they had been unfairly treated in comparison with male counterparts who were promoted to senior equity status. The principal grounds of the claim related to patterns of referrals of work and the consequential disadvantage in billings suffered by the applicants and the reaction of the firm to a request for part-time working. One comment of the Employment Appeal Tribunal to be noted carefully is:

> It is not disputed by and large women have the greater responsibility for child-care in our society and that as a consequence a considerably larger proportion of women than men are unable to commit themselves to full-time working.

It would clearly be a risk for any firm now to take the view that partnership is a full-time commitment only.

Health and safety

Requirement for a policy

The Health and Safety at Work etc. Act 1974 makes it compulsory for every organisation employing five people or more to have a written health and safety policy. There are prosecutions for failure to adopt policies every year and the effects of adverse publicity of a law firm falling foul of such well-established law should be readily apparent. More common are prosecutions for failure to implement safe systems or 'arrangements' of working. Small firms that do not employ so many as five employees should still have a policy since they have the same legal responsibilities to ensure the health and safety of employees and visitors, even if they are exempt from the need to put this into writing.

The advice of the Health and Safety Executive is that somebody who understands the business should draft or at least be involved in the drafting of the policy. The key elements are usually regarded as being the general statement of a commitment to provide a safe working environment for partners, employees and visitors, along with a description of the organisation and its activities. It is important that this policy is kept under regular review. The law does not specify how frequently this should happen since much will depend on the particular activities of the organisation in question, but an annual review is commonly accepted as being appropriate in the absence of unusual factors. Within Lexcel the requirement for a health and safety policy is to be found at section 1.12, while the need for a review is contained in the section dealing with office facilities at section 4.2. To emphasise the importance of such areas not being simply a paper exercise there is a requirement at section 4.2 that the review, which should be conducted no less frequently than annually, must have received consideration by 'top management' – the partners in most firms or perhaps the executive board in substantial practices and in-house departments.

There are four components to a safety policy:

- the general statement – the commitment to ensure a safe working environment;
- the organisation of health and safety – who has management responsibility;
- arrangements for safety – the procedures in place following risk assessments that have been conducted;
- processes for regular reviews.

Responsibility for the policy

The issue of responsibility for the safety policy is often overlooked but does need to be stated. The best approach is to say that all personnel share responsibility for safety but that certain named individuals such as the 'competent person' have management responsibility. The duties of employees are set out in the 1974 Act at ss.7 and 8 and are:

- to take reasonable care of their own health and safety and of others who might be affected by their actions;
- to co-operate with management in relation to its legal responsibilities;
- not to interfere with or misuse any equipment provided for safety purposes.

The need to appoint a 'competent person' arises from the Management of Health and Safety at Work Regulations 1999, SI 1999/3242 (MHSWR). Although this individual should ideally have received training in health and safety they might qualify for the role without it. The competent person would usually be designated as having supervisory responsibility for issues of health and safety and should also be involved in the training that should occur. It will usually be for the competent person to bring the safety policy to the attention of all within the organisation. This will usually be achieved by having the policy and procedures in the office manual, by staff training and perhaps notices about the building and ensuring that health and safety issues form part of the firm's induction training process.

Any safety responsibilities should be reflected in the job descriptions required by section 5.2 in Lexcel – now extended to cover partners, unlike previous versions of the standard where they could be confined to employed staff only.[1] The most specific elements of health and safety for any given firm will be the arrangements for controlling health and safety risks in the practice. There will need to be a combination of inspection procedures, maintenance procedures, training and monitoring.

Risk assessment

The concept of a general risk assessment was also introduced by the MHSWR and should form part of the arrangements required by the safety policy. The aim of this process is to identify the whole range of risks, if possible, that present themselves. Only the more significant of these need to be recorded in writing for those firms that have to have a written policy, though it would be good practice to do so in all firms.

Arising from the general risk assessment there may need to be a series of more specific risk assessments that depend on the nature of the working environment in question. It may well be true that, as the *Lexcel Office*

Procedures Manual provides,[2] there are few risks that are present in a legal office that are not familiar risks in most domestic households but most accidents happen in the home. Tripping dangers are commonplace, especially in busy and overcrowded offices. Instances of serious injuries as people fall into desks or when unstable filing cabinets topple over have been reported and should be taken seriously. Such ever-present risks illustrate the need for all the following elements of health and safety arrangements:

- inspection – where are the danger points from files, cables or floor height variations?
- procedures – who is at risk and what minimum standards should reasonably be established?
- maintenance – are requirements being met? Would a change of floor surface or filing arrangement be appropriate?
- training – what staff instructions might help to gain better compliance?
- monitoring – for example, are standards being met and are tripping incidents being avoided?

Most firms have made adjustments in relation to the risks of eye strain and repetitive strain injury from computer use. Where they have not done so, the provision of eye tests at the firm's expense, the enforcement of regular breaks in activities and commissioning expert advice on work station layout and positioning should all be considered.

Data protection and computer use

Requirement for a plan

The whole area of computer use and the related obligations arising from data protection law form a significant new element of management responsibility. In Lexcel section 4.4 there is now a requirement for an IT plan showing:

a: Responsibility for IT purchasing, installation, maintenance, support and training.
b: The current and planned applications within the practice of IT.
c: A data protection compliance statement in relation to staff, clients and others and registration with the Information Commissioner.
d: Compliance with all appropriate regulations and requirements.
e: User safety [. . .]
f: Appropriate use of e-mail and attachments, both externally and internally, including storage of messages and the implications of not observing such procedures.

g: Computer data and system back up, to the extent not covered in any disaster recovery plan.

Since section 4.2 provides that the above areas 'should' feature in a plan, failure to cover all of the above might not amount to a non-compliance. It may not be necessary, for example, for a sole practitioner to record that he or she has responsibility for purchasing. In most cases, however, firms will need to show that they have covered all or at least most of these issues.

There might have been an argument for not having an IT plan until just a few years ago, but this would seem questionable in all but the small-est and least sophisticated practices now. With ever-increasing numbers of people expecting to communicate by e-mail rather than the traditional postal service, and with plans for the implementation of e-conveyancing now at an advanced stage, firms can no longer avoid the issue of increased computer use.

Initial considerations include responsibility for the management and purchasing of IT facilities. Firms are well advised to plan their applica-tions first and identify possible suppliers and installations second. In addition to use of the more obvious functions of finance and time record-ing data, many practices are at an interesting stage of their development now with a move to case management software in relation to fee earning work. This can be a boon for risk management since such software will often build in compulsory functions that form part of the quality or risk procedures. This will commonly include logging all necessary client details and confirmation of terms for professional compliance, with over-ride possible only in very limited circumstances. Given the risks of exceeding estimates or other costs information provided to clients, the availability of an automatic alert of a costs level being approached is a very useful feature.

Effect of increased use of IT on working patterns

The greater use of e-mail communication in place of traditional postal services has freed up communication for fee earners and enabled them to provide a quicker and more responsive service. This is not all good news, however. Ease of communication out also means ease of communication in, and many practitioners have seen stress levels rise as clients become more demanding in relation to the volume of information provided to their advisers and the expectation of ever-quicker replies. A common complaint is that there is less thinking time, with the risk that the quality of advice may suffer in the rush to respond. The bad practice of yesteryear of consistently sending a fax on the day that the letter was put into the post has been replaced with the phone enquiry – 'you've had my e-mail earlier today – why haven't you responded?'

A practical issue of time management arises from the fact that e-mails will continue to be received throughout the day (and much of the night also in international work). Whereas the mainstay of time management training used to be to develop a routine for the day based around the post received that morning and tasks that were known about already, there is no clear starting point for the daily routine for growing numbers of practitioners. The challenge is to find new patterns of work that maintain productiveness and efficiency. The consequence of not doing so is that the risk of errors is enhanced. Particular problems emerging from increased computer use include:

- the instantaneous nature of e-mails and the ease of reply. A quick response might be a poor response and, if fired off in anger, could lead to a charge of unprofessional conduct;
- failure to check attachments – an increasingly common cause of problems reported to insurers. In one case a client sent a large number of documents by attachment to assist the lawyer, who promptly forwarded them in error to the other side, clearly compromising the client's position in so doing.

Monitoring e-mail and Internet usage

There is a particular need for policies in relation to e-mail and Internet usage. An argument raged for some time as to whether employers could inspect the staff e-mails if they knew that the e-mails were being used in part for personal messages. On the one hand it seemed fair that employers should check messages being passed over their plant and equipment and composed in time paid by for them, but on the other this seemed to breach rights of privacy emerging from new law in the area of human rights. Various statutory provisions continue to have a bearing on this difficult issue. They are:

- Regulation of Investigatory Powers Act 2000;
- Telecommunications (Lawful Business Practice) (Interception of Communications) Regulations 2000, SI 2000/2699; and
- Human Rights Act 1998.

Practices would be well advised to monitor usage by staff since if they do not do so they could be liable for any improper or illegal uses. A very difficult situation could arise if an employee were downloading illegal pornography from the Internet, for example, and the firm had done nothing to prohibit this. To protect itself from a charge that it is now the possessor of the material the firm would need to show that it had prohibited this use in the first place and taken steps to make this clear to all personnel. In order to check for compliance, occasional monitoring would be necessary. The Code of Practice from the Information Commissioner, *The Employment Practices Data Protection Code: Part 3: Monitoring at Work* was published in 2003. Compliance with both the statutory provisions and the Code is essential if a firm wishes to show that it is conducting its monitoring lawfully. The Code imposes on employers a duty to inform employees of monitoring activity and the purpose of it. The Code recommends that any proposed monitoring should be the subject of an 'impact assessment' to decide if and how to carry out the monitoring, balancing the reasons, the potential adverse impact and any alternative solutions.

In respect of monitoring, the emerging principles appear to be that any monitoring must, of course, be lawful. The response should be proportionate to the risk involved. In general, the intrusion should be kept to a minimum and there should be a published policy of which all employees must be aware. What exactly amounts to a 'proportionate' response will be for the organisation to decide. Where possible, monitoring of traffic is preferable to monitoring of content, and automated monitoring is considered less intrusive than targeted monitoring.

The following steps are suggested.

1. Any policy or protocol should be in writing – and communicated to all staff.
2. The rights and obligations in respect of use of e-mail should be clearly stated.
3. Prohibited uses and applications should be specifically stated.
4. Any steps to be taken to monitor staff should be clearly defined.
5. Any privacy rules to be observed should be clearly stated.
6. Any disciplinary sanctions for failing to comply with the established policy should be specified.

In early 2004 the Law Society produced and distributed to all firms guidance and sample policies on these important topics. Practices would be well advised to check their procedures against this publication – the *Lexcel Office Procedures Manual* also contains useful checklists on issues for consideration in the development of appropriate policies.

Data protection compliance

The need to register with the Information Commissioner is referred to in Lexcel with its requirement for a 'documented procedure' for data protection compliance at section 1.11. There are exemptions from the need to register, but it is unlikely that these would apply to many firms given the financial data that is stored in client records. It was reported in late

2002 that only 25 per cent of law firms had then registered as required under the Data Protection Act 1998, which was hardly a ringing endorsement for the profession but the picture is apparently now much improved. Beyond the issue of registration the eight data protection principles that apply to all organisations under the 1998 Act are that data shall be:

- fairly and lawfully processed;
- processed for limited purposes;
- adequate, relevant and not excessive;
- accurate;
- not kept longer than necessary;
- processed in accordance with the data subjects' rights;
- secure;
- not transferred to countries outside the European Economic Area without adequate protection.

The principles have many points of significance in relation to client and staff records and therefore need to be a general consideration in the operation of the firm, especially in the areas of marketing and staff records.

Business continuity

Requirement for a plan

Every firm should have a plan to enable it to trade through an adverse event or circumstance that may temporarily or permanently prevent it from fulfilling its business objectives. A plan is in effect recommended by the Lexcel standard at section 4.3 – the use of the word 'should' indicating that this is an optional element of the standard.

> There should be a business continuity plan envisaging the nature of catastrophic events that could beset the practice and the contingency plans that should be put into effect should they become necessary.

Interestingly, the new draft Rule 5 includes a responsibility to ensure 'the continuation of the practice of the firm in the event of temporary absences and emergencies, with the minimum of interruption to clients' business'. This would therefore go one step further and make some sort of business continuity planning mandatory.

Section 4.4 of the Lexcel standard, dealing with the issues that should appear in an IT plan, talks of a 'disaster recovery plan'. However the document is styled the objective will be much the same – to ensure that an acceptable standard of service delivery is maintained notwithstanding the occurrence of an incident involving the service provider. Such incidents may be catastrophic, such as the total destruction of the office premises, or merely an interruption, such as access to the premises being denied for a period of time. Examples could include a police cordon, a utilities failure, or a water leak rendering the whole or part of the premises unusable.

> EXAMPLE   **Business interruption due to fire at adjoining premises**
>
> One firm was located above a fast food shop, which caught fire. The blaze was put out but not before the firm's offices had been severely damaged by smoke and water. The water had caused the electricity to short out and destroy IT data and had also damaged a large proportion of the files beyond repair. Furthermore, clients who were completing transactions that day were unable to contact the firm and had no idea what was happening. The firm never really recovered and was subsequently taken over by another practice.

Contents of the plan

Business interruption is a risk that has to be managed much like any other risk. The plan should first deal with the possible problems that realistically may be encountered. The firm should consider both the severity of impact and the probability of occurrence. It should be remembered when considering this that the temporary closure of an office might be just as devastating to the practice as if the office were destroyed if there are no plans in place. It is important also to have a structure in place for management in such situations. This should include the appointment of a person in overall charge of business continuity and all staff knowing who this individual is.

The precise structure is likely to be dictated by the size of the firm. The plan needs to set out clearly how staff should respond to such an incident. (One member of a firm on being asked what he would do if he could not gain access to the firm said he would probably get a game of golf in.) The plan must be drafted to meet the specific situation of the firm taking into account its premises, IT use, work types and spread of personnel. Precedents are helpful but should not be followed blindly.

The plan should address the following:

- a list of suppliers of essential goods together with contact details;
- contact home and mobile telephone numbers of key personnel in the firm;

- details of location of alternative premises and who should attend at those premises;
- details of offsite IT servers and backup facilities;
- 24-hour contact details of insurers or brokers.

Staff should be supplied with numbers to contact in the event of a problem and should be trained in how to respond. The plan should not be overly detailed since it needs to be easy to understand and follow. Key personnel must have access to the plan outside the office environment. Past experience has revealed that often those in positions of authority were unable to function effectively because they had left their copy of the plan in the office.

Implementing and reviewing the plan

Once the plan is in place it should be tested. One useful exercise is to contact all key personnel as identified in the plan in as short a period of time as possible. An exercise should be undertaken to see how quickly the alternative premises can be set up to function effectively. Evacuation procedures should also be tested in case the firm does receive notice of the need to vacate its premises – who would take what and how would client confidentiality be maintained?

The plan should be treated as a 'living document' and be kept under constant review. Often a firm's business continuity plan is filed away and forgotten about. This raises the risk of the plan failing when it is activated by reason of an incident. One plan provided for relocation of the IT department to premises that had been demolished several months prior to the incident and were currently being redeveloped by new owners. It is worth reiterating that all firms should have the facility to backup information off site, or at least arrange for the information to be taken off site manually at the end of each working day.

Insurance

Finally, practices should look closely at their insurance arrangements in respect of business interruption. In the event of an incident occurring the firm must have adequate levels of cover in place. The firm must be aware that considerable additional costs over and above the cover provided are likely to be incurred, such as managing the implementation of the plan in the event of an incident.

Notes

1   Section D1 in the 2000 version of Lexcel on job descriptions and section D4.b in relation to performance appraisals.
2   M. Moore (ed.), *Lexcel Office Procedures Manual*, Law Society Publishing, 2004 (hereafter in this book referred to as *Lexcel Office Procedures Manual*), p.56.

5

Supervision

Introduction

Risk management can be seen as the art of anticipating and preventing errors. There is an argument that all errors in the office environment are ultimately human since people will always be involved, whatever the process. It is useful in the legal context, however, to distinguish between human errors and failures of office systems. A time limit is missed, for example. Either there is no system in place to prevent this happening or someone has failed to apply the system correctly. It should follow that supervision and checking will always need to form a component of any risk management system – human errors will continue to be a fact of life in even the best designed systems. Not surprisingly, supervision also features in all the main quality management systems.

Beyond the realms of risk and quality management, supervision also makes good business sense. Income may be generated by fee earning hours, but profit is also based on gearing – the extent to which employed fee earners can be deployed to provide services to clients. Where gearing is low and the firm is partner-heavy, good levels of profit can only be expected if the firm performs premium work that will support high fee rates. Whatever the practice, profits will be maximised where there can be as broad a base as possible to a pyramid of staff to partners. This concept is best illustrated by the accountant trainer Robert Mowbray as:

$$
\begin{aligned}
\text{Profit per partner} \quad = \quad &\text{Gearing (number of fee earners per partner)} \\
&\times \text{ annual chargeable hours recorded per fee} \\
& \text{ earner} \\
&\times \text{ average charge-out rate per fee earner} \\
&\times \text{ recovery (percentage of work in progress} \\
& \text{ billed and recovered)} \\
&\times \text{ margin (i.e. take away expenses)}
\end{aligned}
$$

Unfortunately, difficulties of recruitment pose a brake in many firms on attempts to implement a strategy for improving profits by increasing gearing. The better the profile of the firm, the more likely it is that talented staff can be attracted into the firm. Sooner or later, however, may come the ultimatum – 'partnership now or I go elsewhere to achieve it'. Where staff have been appointed supervision then becomes key to maintaining quality and service while minimising risk. Junior personnel who lack the experience of seniors are likely to make more errors: this will impact on the service provided to clients and thus the reputation of the firm and its risk profile. Effective supervision should be seen as an essential ingredient for managing the risk implicit in the contribution of less experienced personnel.

Solicitors' Practice Rules

The obligation on solicitors to ensure that their practices are subject to effective supervision has steadily increased. The earliest versions of Practice Rule 13 tended to look merely at the need for all offices to have one individual qualified to supervise but this has progressively been broadened. A new version of the Rule dating from 1999 introduced the concept of some compulsory management training for those who were deemed to be office supervisors but the effect was limited by allowing a 10-year phasing-in period. Even then, the training was limited to a requirement of just 12 hours, apparently planned primarily as attendance on the Law Society's Management Course, Stages 1 and 2.

The requirement in the current Practice Rule 13 to ensure that the practice is appropriately supervised and managed appears in similar terms in the proposed Rule 5. This is stated to deal with the 'supervision and management of a firm or in-house practice, the maintenance of competence, and the internal business arrangements essential to the proper delivery of services to clients'. The Rule relates to two of the new core duties in the proposed Rule 1 – 1.09 on management and 1.06 on competence. Rule 5.01 provides that those in charge of the firm must make proper arrangements for compliance with their legal duties and regulatory obligations, as well as arrangements for:

- adequate supervision and direction of clients' matters;
- effective management for the firm as a whole;
- client care arrangements;
- training to ensure competence;
- identification of conflicts of interest;
- continuation of the practice during absences and emergencies;
- safekeeping of documentation and assets entrusted to the firm;
- avoidance of discrimination;
- compliance with the Money Laundering Regulations, where appropriate;
- financial controls;
- control of undertakings;
- risk management.

This list of responsibilities is very much more detailed than the equivalent provisions in Practice Rule 13 which it is intended to replace. Rule 5.02 retains the long-established rule that at least one principal in the practice should have held a practising certificate for at least 36 months but applications to waive this are still possible under the guidance to the proposed Rule 5.

As to the terminology there are also some helpful definitions in note (b) to Practice Rule 13, with supervision being seen as:

> the professional overseeing of staff and the professional overseeing of clients' matters.

while 'management' is seen more generally as:

> a wider concept, which encompasses the overall direction and development of the practice and its day-to-day control and administration. Management functions include business efficiency as well as professional competence.

Lexcel

Within Lexcel the requirements on supervision appear in section 6 alongside the provisions dealing with operational risk management.

Organisational structures

They start with an analysis of structures – everyone should know where they fit into the supervisory structure. Section 6.1 refers to the need for a written description of the management structure that designates the responsibilities of individuals and their accountability. Any changes must be updated within three months. In practice most firms will satisfy this either by the adoption of an organisational chart or by a simple description of the departmental arrangements in the office manual.

Named supervisors

Section 6.2 sets out the requirement for a 'named supervisor for each area of work undertaken by the practice'. There is sometimes confusion about this requirement and its relationship to Practice Rule 13 or the draft Rule 5. The professional rules concentrate on having one person in each firm who is 'qualified to supervise'. The quality standards tend to pick up on the concept at a more everyday level and examine whether the supervision of individual matters is effective. The criteria by which this is judged in Lexcel are that each supervisor needs to have 'appropriate experience' of the work supervised and should also be able to 'guide and assist others'. It should be noted that there is very little by way of prescription on this in Lexcel, in which respect the Law Society's standard is in marked contrast to the legal aid standard – the SQM. That standard expects a supervisor to meet technical requirements by being on a specialist panel (if one exists) and maintaining at least 350 hours per year in that area of practice. Where there is no panel, as in housing work, the supervisors will need to submit and maintain a 'portfolio' of work showing the experience they have in that area of work. This may seem preferable to the more permissive Lexcel standard but has been one of the principal causes of the decline in the availability of legal aid services in many regions. Rural areas have been particularly badly hit by these requirements. In certain of the less mainstream contract areas, such as consumer and contract law, it is unlikely that any one practitioner will be able to maintain an adequate supply of instructions to continue to meet the requirements. The Legal Services Commission has been well aware of this problem over the years but has remained committed to the requirements. Some leeway is provided under 'tolerance' arrangements, under which a firm may be allowed to commence a limited number of 'matter starts' in areas where it holds no contract. The probability, however, is that the service ceases to be offered and shortages become a problem.

A further problem of over-prescription in the qualifications of supervisors is that it can mean that firms are unduly inhibited in their ability to develop a new service. It is interesting to explore with many firms how and when a particular expertise developed. Often it is a chance set of novel instructions that has opened up an avenue of practice development to everyone's advantage. As long as the firm can show that it has met its professional obligations in providing a service only where it had the necessary resources to do so there is nothing improper in this. Over-prescription can lead to the 'catch 22' situation where there is a clear demand for a service but an inability of firms to develop to meet it.

Controlled and well-managed development needs to be possible and should be in everyone's best interests.

Supervision to be 'effective'

Beyond the need for an organisational structure and named supervisors Lexcel requires that supervision of both the staff (section 6.3) and the legal work undertaken (section 6.4) are 'effective'. The use of this word in both provisions is deliberate and places the emphasis on whether the arrangements adopted by a firm actually work. Although the wording of both sections provides illustrations of the kind of supervisory steps a firm might consider there is little in the way of mandatory provisions – the acid test is simply whether the steps taken by that firm or department actually work. The best evidence that the arrangements are appropriate is a dearth of complaints, claims and errors observed on assessment.

The illustrative lists in Lexcel are useful in considering what supervision would be appropriate in any given situation.

Checks on incoming and outgoing post, including e-mails and faxes (section 6.3a)

The checking of incoming post is a near universal safeguard in law firms and is a practical check on what is going on in the firm. It is not a professional requirement as such and an earlier, somewhat ambivalent reference to it in the 1990 version of Practice Rule 13 has now been removed:

> In determining whether or not there has been compliance with the require-ment as to supervision . . . account shall be taken of, *inter alia*, the arrangements for principals to see incoming mail.
>
> Practice Rule 13(2) – now repealed

Unfortunately, the effectiveness of checking incoming post has become more limited in any event since so much more communication is now by electronic means. The feasibility of checking incoming e-mails has been examined in Chapter 4. Various arrangements for post checking are encountered in practice, from the heavy burden of the supervisor being copied in on every message to and from one of their team to a requirement that every e-mail sent and received is printed out in hard copy and placed along with all correspondence in front of the supervisor on the file for subsequent checking. Balance is needed on the issue. The arrangement chosen has to be practicable and appropriate or the checker will lose interest and morale will suffer. One of the underlying principles of supervisory management is that people need to be encouraged to take responsibility for their actions, so it might be advisable to limit checking of all post and messages for a limited, probationary period. It is a problem observable in firms where checking by seniors continues longer than elsewhere that fee earners do not always take as much care as they should with their work since they know the correspondence will be checked in any event.

The arrangements for checking incoming faxes may reduce in importance as use of that communication method declines, but it is a weakness in many firms that incoming post might be checked carefully but that later faxes and hand deliveries escape the process. A fax, being a more immediate method of communication, might be used in preference to the post where there is some urgency or irritation on the part of the sender and there are therefore grounds for checking faxes more carefully than normal correspondence. In many firms a junior will hand a copy of any fax to a partner or at least place a copy of it in their in-tray in the general office for later inspection.

Departmental, team and office meetings and communication structures (section 6.3b)

Meetings may be the continuing scourge of office life in most areas of business but tend to be more carefully rationed in the fee earning environment of the law firm. If anything, firms could often benefit from giving greater emphasis to the need to conduct regular team meetings and insist on attendance at them as a matter of importance. The effectiveness of any meeting is compromised where one or two members of the department fail to appear on grounds of having to see a client. This stems from seeing the meeting as a secondary and rather unimportant activity. It is very unlikely that the same fee earners would have cancelled other client appointments to see the clients in question. The meeting should be seen to be at least as important as a client appointment.

It does need to be recognised, however, that time at a meeting is time out of the fee earning day and this means that the meeting should always be clearly planned in advance and well conducted on the day. The frequency of meetings will determine the agenda. A weekly meeting will tend to concentrate on diary checking, especially in areas of litigation where court dates need attention – crime most obviously. A monthly meeting is more the norm and can deal with issues of business performance – targets for hours and bills, for example, as well as practice development and personnel issues. Many departments provide the opportunity to discuss workloads at meetings of this nature and encourage attendees to request help with or reallocation of work. In some firms it is a condition of going on an external training course or conference that the fee earner should be prepared to give a brief presentation on the most important points to emerge from the day, while firms that subscribe to video-based training might take the opportunity to show a recent programme if it is relevant. In both cases people at meetings might be able to count attendance for some or all the meeting for Continuing Professional Development (CPD) purposes, especially if the firm has an in-house authorisation agreement in place with the Law Society.[1]

Whatever the type or frequency of meeting it is a good principle to keep matters to a short and well-defined agenda. When people know that they can rely on the meeting finishing on time they are more likely to support it. If the right balance is struck between reporting and discussion the meeting should have a positive effect on morale. Another useful tip is not to rely on formal minutes. Minutes that emerge several days or even weeks after the event can be a great excuse for inactivity – better by far to make handwritten notes of the main items discussed and the decisions made and copy these to everyone concerned at the end of the meeting.

The type of communication structures that will be appropriate for any given practice, like so many things, will depend on the firm in question. By and large, face-to-face communication is more likely to be believed than written edicts. In an increasing number of firms there is an annual presentation by the management board or partner to report to the firm on performance and to record thanks to all for their contribution. The Investors in People standard has always laid particular emphasis on communicating the strategy of the practice to those within the firm and this now appears most obviously as the evidence statement that:

> Managers can describe how they involve people when developing the organ-isation's business plan and when agreeing team and individual objectives.
>
> IIP, 1.4

Most firms are very much more open with staff than they used to be. The higher uptake of limited liability partnerships has lessened the financial secrecy that has accompanied even the more open of firms. Accounts have to be filed under the legislation that enables partnerships to have limited liability, making the financial statements public documents in larger firms that are not exempt from the provisions. The experience of most is that a virtuous circle develops, whereby greater staff involvement promotes enhanced motivation and this in turn promotes greater morale and a better service to clients. Properly managed, there should be a business improvement from a more open style of supervision.

Reviews of matter print-outs in order to ensure good financial controls and the appropriate allocation of workloads (section 6.3c)

Regular reviews of the data on matter print-outs can go beyond good financial housekeeping and can be a useful supervisory step in themselves. This is particularly the case with section 6.5 of Lexcel, which requires procedures to be in place to ensure fee earners consider their matters regularly to maintain progress. If the report shows the number of weeks or months lapsed since time last recorded on the matters this should satisfy this relatively new requirement.[2]

The exercise of devolved powers in publicly funded work (section 6.3d)

In certain areas of publicly funded work firms are expected to make decisions that formerly would have been made by the legal aid authorities – the issue of emergency funding being one of the most common examples. The Legal Services Commission expects proper safeguards to be in place when such decisions are made and there can be penalties for firms for inappropriate decisions. Legal aid firms will therefore generally find the consideration of the use of devolved powers to be a useful opportunity to exercise a supervisory review on the matter in question.

Independent file reviews

Independent file reviews form a mandatory element of the Lexcel standard and an important component of any strategy to improve supervision. File reviews are generally seen as a random, sampling exercise. If reviewers are hoping to discover every error in the filing cabinet of the person checked they are likely to be disappointed. What they should instead expect is to gain an appreciation of this person's style of working and a sense of whether he or she follows the necessary procedures. Both Lexcel and the SQM expect the designated supervisor to conduct or be involved in the file review process and both standards also require an occasional examination of file reviews to see what trends and data emerge. Lexcel allows the firm to determine the frequency and depth of the reviews but an assessor would not accept arrangements that were clearly inadequate. The SQM, likewise, claims that firms can determine the frequency and number of files but the guidance document that forms part of the SQM 2002 provides an illustrative table (at p.77), the provisions of which many auditors expect to be adopted. At section 6.6c Lexcel states that this review will need to contribute to the annual risk assessment report required under the operational risk management provisions at section 6.7f. Generally file reviews should be both substantive and procedural but there is an option to make them procedural only; this is more obviously relevant where there is one specialist only in the firm and it would not be feasible for any other person in the practice to take a view on the appropriateness and accuracy of the advice and service given. It is important that any 'corrective action' required by the reviewer does occur and is then signed off.

All too often file reviews are seen as one of the most unwelcome chores of running a quality or risk management system. With a little imagination it need not be so. There is no reason why, as most firms seem to think, file reviews must be an activity confined to the last Friday in the month with a line through the diary for the whole afternoon. If the objective is to gain a picture of the files managed by a colleague file reviews could be an ongoing activity to be considered whenever there is a conference or discussion on the best way forward on a particular matter. If noted as such at the time, in both the matter file and the central file review record required by Lexcel and the SQM, this can count towards the data that will be required by the file review procedures.

In many firms the right procedures might be in place and the office manual may say the right things, but this will not necessarily mean that supervision works as well as it should. The most common reason for disappointment with the supervisory arrangements is that those charged to supervise do not place enough priority on the role. It is a rather familiar problem that fee earners prefer to get on with their own work whenever possible and see any additional responsibilities, most typically supervision of others or marketing the department, as unimportant or peripheral. Supervision, rather like client care, has to be a matter of attitude, skills and systems. Section 6 of Lexcel concentrates on the systems needed to supervise others effectively, but unless these systems are accompanied by proper commitment disappointment is likely. There are many supervisors who continue to believe in a 'sink or swim' mentality whereby juniors are judged to be up to or below standard on the basis of an isolated incident. Supervision training can also be useful in showing the importance of continuing to work with those charged to control others and how to do so. Only then will firms be likely to achieve the results hoped for by improving supervision within the practice.

Delegation

Delegation is a daily and necessary activity wherever supervision is a consideration. Sadly, delegation in law firms is often disappointing for both delegator and delegatee. Most groups of trainees will recount situations of being sent along to court to make difficult applications on a complex matter where they have no understanding of the issues in hand and have received little by way of any briefing. Another common example is the request to supervise the conveyancing department in the trainee's first weeks in the firm while the partner is on holiday. An increasingly common complaint is the instructions being limited to 'please deal' on the ubiquitous yellow stickie on the file.

Delegators, on the other hand, will complain that by the time they have explained what needs doing, waited for it to be done and checked and rechecked the efforts of others they could have done the job quicker themselves.

The main difficulty of law firm delegation seems to be one of trust and involvement. Mistakes, whether great or small, matter in the law. This can encourage the practitioner to do all or nothing on any given file. They will accept the blame for their mistakes, but not others'. This can in turn encourage the development of perfectionist tendencies. The perfectionist will want things done their way: delegation requires the acceptance that others may have a different style or approach that could be equally valid. Mistakes are one thing, but variations in style and approach should be another. The danger is also that any sense of commerciality in delegation is lost. The delegator who prefers to rewrite what has been submitted to them rather than accept the efforts of the delegatee has undermined the usual reason for delegation – to get the work done more cost-effectively at the appropriate level.

The first step towards better delegation is therefore to review the standards expected of others. If the expectation is that work will always be done to the standard and in the manner that the supervisor expects, some compromise may be needed. This compromise should not extend to matters of right and wrong or to firm-wide style, but should apply to other related details. Supervisors should accept that if they want the work done their way they may well have to do it themselves, but if they want to relieve the pressure they are experiencing and meet their obligation to develop others they may have to accept that others might have a different approach.

The delegator should always make it clear who has responsibility for the file itself and for the various tasks associated with it. There should be no confusion over such critical issues as who has the main responsibility for client contact or whose job it is to ensure that progress is maintained. Requiring the inexperienced delegatee to have checks before critical steps in the progression of the instructions will be a sensible precaution. As the delegatee's experience grows the need for checking should also reduce.

A useful checklist when delegating is:

- What   Establish what needs to be done.
- Why   Understanding context will generally help.
- When   A deadline should always be agreed.
- Time   As long as it takes or should efforts be limited?
- Authority   Authorise dealings with the client or opposition.
- Resources   Indicate what other files or drafts might help.

The provision of continual feedback should be seen to be an important part of the delegation process. Either the job has been done well enough, in which case this should be acknowledged, or there is some shortcoming. Where the task was not performed well enough it is important that this is pointed out to the delegatee as constructively as possible. Ideally an opportunity to repeat the task should also be found as soon as possible after this conversation.

'Hard' and 'soft' delegation

It is helpful to draw a distinction between 'hard' and 'soft' delegation. In hard delegation the delegatee has the necessary skills and experience to do the work in question. This is the best option for the supervisor as the time taken to explain the task should not be too great and the prospects of the job being performed correctly are enhanced. Quality checks might be worked in: perhaps the supervisor should check the work when it is ready to be sent out or receive confirmation that the work has been done. Nonetheless, the supervisor should have confidence that all will happen as it should.

In soft delegation the delegatee does not have the necessary skills and experience to do the work in question – typically it will involve the trainee who has recently joined the department and who has not performed this task previously. A number of difficulties arise for the supervisor, not least the time it will take to have the work done this way. By the time the supervisor has have provided a full explanation of what needs to be done, checked it when it is submitted and then awaited the corrected item, the conclusion could easily be that 'it would have been quicker to do it myself'. True enough, but if the trainee does not have the opportunity to learn on the way the firm is not investing in its future ability to pass work to experienced personnel.

Better delegation comes from always being clear why delegation is occurring. If the aim is to have the work done cost-effectively, hard delegation techniques will be appropriate, but expecting work to be done correctly with minimal supervision from someone who should be a soft delegation target is only likely to cause problems. Above all, delegation of tasks should not be seen as an abdication of responsibility – a view supported by the wording of the proposed Rule 5.

Personnel systems

The role of personnel management systems in supervision should not be overlooked. The terms under which staff are employed amount to a form of control over the work of the firm and are the subject of section 5 in the Lexcel standard: 'People management'. Lexcel 2004 introduces the need for some element of personnel planning – an optional exercise in earlier versions of the standard: The plan must cover 'the recruitment, development and welfare' of personnel but can be covered wherever the firm feels most appropriate – in many practices it will be dealt with as part of an annual departmental development planning exercise.

Job description

Job descriptions are an important requirement under section 5.2 of Lexcel. The need for job descriptions now extends to all personnel and thus extends to partners as well as staff. It is an error to see creation of job descriptions as being merely an administrative task to be ticked off the list of what has to be done under Lexcel and, where relevant, the SQM (SQM 2002, section D1.1). The job description is an opportunity to settle any points of confusion over what exactly is expected of the jobholder. Some argue that maximum flexibility is best for the firm and that the job documentation should be as vague as possible, but others see the same paperwork as being one of the prime tools for clarifying who does what when the whole process of fee earning is being examined. The *Lexcel Office Procedures Manual* provides a number of precedent job descriptions, including a draft paralegal document detailing the specific tasks that the jobholder might undertake as part of their fee earning contribution.

The job description is always a useful point of reference for existing personnel and should be used by more firms as part of the annual appraisal or review process. It is also key to improving the quality of decisions made in the recruitment process. Recruitment and selection work best where they are as objective as possible and the early drafting of a detailed job description can serve to clarify what is expected by both employer and employee.

Appraisals

The requirements in relation to appraisals now extend to partners as well as employed staff, as they have done for those undertaking legal aid work under the SQM for some time.[3] There have been considerable developments in appraisal systems since law firms first started adopting them at the end of the 1980s, with the whole process now becoming less judgmental and more forward-looking. Many firms have abandoned ratings schemes in place of comments-only schemes. Likewise, more firms have introduced 'upward' review schemes where staff are asked for their views on how they are supervised and '360 degree' schemes that add other sources of data such as client feedback to ensure as wide and as accurate a picture as possible of the person under review. A partner review process is now required under section 5.7a of Lexcel and an increasing number of larger firms are linking such schemes to some limited amount of performance-based profit sharing.

Although not essential as such, it is difficult to see how most organisations would satisfy the Investors in People standard without a review scheme that functions well. The appraisal scheme will be the usual way in which training needs are discussed and agreed, the idea being that all training should be relevant in some way to wider objectives in the organisation or the team that the individual belongs to. Section 5.8 of Lexcel provides that training should be provided in accordance with the policy on training and development. A review of whether training undertaken did actually meet the needs that had been identified is always advisable – forms for the purpose can be found in the *Lexcel Office Procedures Manual.*

Induction training

The only other element of people management covered in section 5 of Lexcel is induction training. This needs to be a process only, meaning that procedures describing what will happen are not necessary. As long as induction can be observed to occur in a satisfactory manner the requirements of the standard will be met. Section 5.5 requires induction to occur within a reasonable time, while under section 5.6 some form of induction is needed when existing personnel transfer roles within the firm.

Notes

1 For details of how to apply for an in-house authorisation agreement, contact the Training Department of the Law Society. A fee is payable.
2 Much the same provision requiring checking for inactivity can be found in the SQM 2002 at section E1.2(e). This envisages quarterly checking at least of files.
3 Partner reviews were first made necessary by the 1998 LAFQAS standard at section J1.4 – the equivalent provisions are to be found in the SQM 2002 at section D2.2.

6

Client acquisition

KEY POINTS _____

- Who is the client?
- What are the instructions?
- Conflict of interest check
- Money laundering checks
- Financial viability
- Expertise and resources
- Previous experience
- Client's expectations
- Reputation
- Risk assessment
- Retainer letters
- Letters of non-engagement

All instructions can be analysed as coming from either established or new clients. Regardless of their source, the firm will always need to consider if this is work that the firm could or should be doing at that point in time. Consideration needs to be given to whether the firm has the expertise and resources to do the work and if other circumstances such as a conflict of interest make the work inappropriate. In situations involving new clients additional considerations arise and thought will be needed as to whether this is a client that the firm wishes to act for. The decision whether to accept work from existing clients is likely to be more straight-forward but it will also be important to consider whether changed circumstances make it inadvisable to act for that client on this occasion.

The processes whereby a firm receives work should be one of its key risk management checks. Perhaps the single most effective step that a firm can take to improve its risk profile is to turn work away that for some reason it should not handle. Time and time again exasperated partners called upon to defend a claim will comment to insurers 'why we accepted this work in the first place is beyond me'. It should be stressed that there is no obligation to accept all instructions from clients, even if of a work type that the firms specialises in. There is no 'cab-rank principle' for solicitors' firms and as long as instructions are not declined on grounds that would be offensive to anti-discrimination policies the firm can choose which instructions it will accept or decline. It should also be borne in mind that whereas prior to accepting instructions the lawyer is generally entitled to decline to act, terminating the retainer at a later stage can be very much more problematic (see Chapter 10, p.136).

In Lexcel the importance of work acceptance is recognised in two procedures that are new to Lexcel 2004 and which are found at the start of section 8, dealing with client and file acceptance. These procedures are also cross-referred to in part at section 6.8a in the standard on the risk elements of taking on new work.

> 8.1 Practices will document how client enquiries in relation to possible instructions are handled, with particular regard to:
>
> a: The treatment of telephone enquiries.
> b: Clients who enquire in person in the reception area, including confidentiality.
> c: Enquiries by correspondence and e-mail.

This procedure is geared very much to the messages that a firm conveys to enquirers as to its efficiency and willingness to do the work. There will be different considerations for a high street practice that draws most of its work from passers-by as opposed to a niche commercial practice that might have minimal reception facilities. Conveyancing departments are likely to recognise the importance of providing swift and helpful responses to requests for quotes from potential clients and will be likely to have specific arrangements in place for this.

> 8.2 Practices will document how decisions will be made whether to accept new instructions from existing clients or instructions from clients who have not instructed the practice before.

This procedure is central to the issue of client vetting. In many firms it often seems that the sole criterion for taking on a particular client is the potential fee income that might be generated from the work that that client will produce. This might be understandable, given the considerable pressure that exists in many firms to meet fee targets. It would clearly be misguided, however, to overlook such issues as whether the client is likely to pay for the services provided and whether existing client relationships could be prejudiced by taking on new clients. It is important that a clear policy is in place – perhaps varying for each department – for decisions to be made as to whether the firm will act. The following elements should form part of this client vetting procedure.

Who is the client?

There can often be confusion as to the precise relationship between adviser and client. The most obvious difficulties stem from a failure to establish the credentials of a representative of an organisation. The adviser will need to be satisfied that this individual has the actual authority to represent the corporation or association that he or she purports to represent. Problems also arise from a failure to see the potential for differing interests at a later stage, especially when things go wrong. The most common problems here arise when a solicitor agrees to act on behalf of a number of family members in relation to one transaction.

> CASE STUDY   **Purchase of a council house: conflict of interest**
>
> A number of claims arose during the last property recession where a lawyer had acted for various members of a family in relation to one transaction. The classic example was the purchase of a council house. Mother and father lived in the property and qualified for the discount. They were retired, however, and could not obtain a mortgage. The son or daughter, perhaps with spouse or partner, seeing a potentially profitable property transaction, would agree to guarantee the mortgage. A brother or sister, not wishing to miss out on the deal, provided the balance of the purchase money. When recession struck and the mortgage guarantor found him or herself out of a job and thus unable to pay the mortgage, the lender took possession. The parents were now out of a home and everyone involved incurred losses from negative equity. The solicitor could be seen to have both acted for and failed everyone involved in the sorry situation without regard to the potential for contrary interests to be considered.

In *Royal Bank of Scotland Plc* v. *Etridge (No.2)* [2001] UKHL 44 the husband instructed solicitors to witness the wife's signature giving effect to postponement of her interest in the matrimonial home in favour of a charge to a bank to secure a loan to a limited company. The decision was the lead case in a series of cases that involved a wife who had charged her interest in the matrimonial home in favour of a financial institution to secure borrowing in favour of the husband or the husband's business. Subsequently, when the wife faced eviction by reason of the husband's business failing and the institution seeking possession, the allegation was made that the document was signed by the wife because of the husband exerting undue influence over her. Frequently in such situations it transpired that the solicitor acted for all the parties. The question of impartial advice and potential conflict was considered by Lord Nicholls in his judgment:

I emphasise, therefore, that in every case the solicitor must consider carefully whether there is any conflict of duty or interest and more widely, whether it would be in the best interests of the wife for him to accept instructions from her. If he decides to accept instructions, his assumption of legal and professional responsibilities to her ought, in the ordinary course of things, to provide sufficient assurance that he will give the requisite advice fully, carefully and conscientiously. Especially so, now that the nature of the advice called for has been clarified. If at any stage the solicitor becomes concerned that there is a real risk that other interests or duties may inhibit his advice to the wife he must cease to act for her.

In some cases it cannot be assumed that the client actually exists. Money laundering client identification checks do need to extend to principals who are represented by agents and the danger of acting for a fictitious client also arises under mortgage fraud provisions.[1] With corporate clients, best practice would dictate that a company search is undertaken in respect of all instructions to make sure that the client still exists. Issuing proceedings on behalf of a limited company in the High Court and running an action for a year, only to find that the company has been struck off the register for failing to file annual returns prior to issue, will expose the lawyer to the potential of a substantial wasted costs order. Along similar lines, there are dangers when acting on an inter-company transaction involving subsidiaries. Transferring a valuable property into the incorrect company's hands can prove to be very costly.

More firms are more likely to be wary as to client identification issues given the need for checks under money laundering provisions. In some firms such checks are not necessarily conducted across the board where it is felt that the Money Laundering Regulations 2003, SI 2003/3075 do not apply to certain areas of work. Whether routine checks are conducted or not all departments should remember the importance of establishing who is the client for reasons more fundamental than money laundering compliance.

Sometimes a letter of non-engagement will be needed to ensure that the client understands that the firm is not acting on behalf of the client. It should eradicate the possibility of there being a misunderstanding between lawyer and client as to what has or has not been agreed. The precise content of the letter will be dictated by the particular circumstances of the matter, but would probably most obviously include such issues as the reason why the instructions have been declined. The firm might stress that although the firm is declining instructions it is not expressing any opinion as to the merits of the case. If there are any impending critical dates such as the exercise of an option, or the expiration of limitation periods, these should be drawn to the attention of the client in general terms. The need to consult another adviser without delay should be stressed. The firm will need to make sure that it returns all papers and documents left by the client and that there is an accessible record of the decision to decline the work, along with a copy of the letter sent to the client for later reference.

What are the instructions?

Having established who the client is, the next step is to obtain clear instructions. This will enable the lawyer to deal with other steps in the client acquisition process including the risk analysis, and also to decide whether the firm has the time, expertise and resources available to meet the client's expectations. It is always preferable, though not technically necessary, to see the client in person. The first interview with the client is the principal opportunity to obtain all the requisite information from the client in order to enable the lawyer to formulate his or her advice. Thereafter the client will be able to make an informed decision as to whether he or she wishes to proceed.

In Lexcel section 8.4 there is a useful summary of the points to be dealt with when taking instructions.

At the outset of the matter the fee-earner will establish:

a: As full an understanding as possible of the client's requirements and objectives (where incomplete this must be supplemented subsequently).
b: A clear explanation of the issues raised and the advice given.
c: What the fee-earner will do and in what timescale.
d: Whether the fee-earner is the appropriate person to deal with the matter or whether it should be referred to a colleague.
e: Method of funding, including the availability or suitability of insurance, trade union benefits, conditional or contingency fee arrangements, or costs insurance products.
f: Whether the intended action would be merited on a cost benefit analysis and whether, in public funding cases, the guidance in the funding code would be satisfied.

The same section goes on to state that the instructions should be confirmed to the client, usually in writing. Some lawyers do this by sending a copy of an attendance note for the client to review but most will send out a letter confirming instructions and another 'client care' letter confirming terms of acting on this occasion.

It may sometimes be that the adviser is able to obtain an unconditional authority in writing to accept instructions from a third party, or from one of several clients. In such a case care should be taken to refer to the current edition of *The Guide to the Professional Conduct of Solicitors* (8th edn, 1999 at the time of writing) (the Guide) and the recommendations in that publication as to how to proceed. In such situations the solicitor must obtain written authority from the client that he or she wishes the solicitor to act, and if the solicitor is any doubt whatsoever the client should be seen. Further, the solicitor must always advise the client without reference to the interests of the third party.

The initial interview will also form the basis for the retainer letter to be sent to the client. A checklist of standard questions may assist so as to ensure all basic issues are addressed. Certain areas of work lend themselves to pro forma instruction sheets more easily than others. In Lexcel there is a provision at section 8.7a that '[k]ey information must be recorded on the file' and checklists will be an excellent way to do this. Not only do such forms make information more accessible to all who use the file but they also ensure that less experienced personnel remember to take instructions on all the important issues.

Many claims against lawyers have been based on confusion as to the precise scope of the retainer. Where a firm declines to take responsibility for an element of the instructions – taxation in transactions is the most common example – this should be clearly stated in the written confirmation to the client. Failure to do so might result in the client claiming that it was reasonable for them to assume that the issue was being dealt with since they were not told otherwise.

Conflict of interest check

A conflicts check must be undertaken as part of the file opening process. Acting for a client where a conflict of interest arises is a breach of Law Society professional conduct rules. Conflicts can, of course, also develop during the course of the retainer and advisers will need to remain alert to this possibility. The issues relating to conflicts are examined in greater detail in Chapter 7.

Money laundering checks

Money laundering identification checks must be undertaken in relation to 'regulated business', subject to the distinction between one-off transactions and business relationships as examined in Chapter 11. Most firms seem to take the view that it is preferable to undertake checks across the board for all work rather than risk the interpretation of the somewhat unclear provisions on the subject in the money laundering regime. Although the Money Laundering Regulations 2003 say that checks should be carried out as soon as is reasonably practicable it is usually advisable to insist on evidence of identification as a precondition of taking instructions. Criminals often work on the basis that if they delay the production of the identification evidence for as long as possible the lawyer will forget or overlook the fact that the evidence has not been obtained. The longer the delay, the greater the risk that this will happen.

Financial viability

Many managing partners and finance directors would put issues as to whether and how the client will pay for services provided at the top of their client vetting list. Short of a clear pro bono policy, there is little point in doing work for which the firm will be unlikely to recover proper payment. While the financial status of the client may at first sight appear to have little to do with operational risk, it does pose a threat. Dissatisfaction with a firm's costs often leads to discontent on the part of the client, which in turn may lead to confrontation. When the solicitor presses for payment difficulties can easily escalate into complaints and claims.

The prospect of non-payment suggests that enquiries should be made as to the viability of the work and the client's financial status. This does not necessarily mean requesting full financial disclosure of the client's means but it should at least involve a cost–benefit analysis with the client in relation to the proposed transaction. The less sophisticated the client is in respect of legal matters the more important this analysis becomes. Most advisers will need little in the way of warning as to the implications of statements such as: 'I don't care how much this costs, it's a matter of principle.' Experience usually shows that such lofty principles often struggle to survive the billing process, interim or final.

Carrying out a cost–benefit analysis may be difficult by reason of the lawyer not actually knowing the level of costs that will be incurred in the transaction. It is, of course, often difficult to assess how much time lawyers will spend on a transaction or dispute. The client is entitled nonetheless to the best information possible on the likely overall costs of the matter and it should always be possible to provide some indication of the level of cost that will be incurred depending on the stage that is reached. The lawyer should then discuss frankly with the client whether it is worth the client pursuing the matter further and ensure that this conversation is fully noted and confirmed to the client. The obligation to ensure that this is dealt with arises under para.4(k) of the Solicitors' Costs Information and Client Care Code 1999, which provides that:

> The solicitor should discuss with the client whether the likely outcome in a matter will justify the risk involved including, if relevant, the risk of having to bear an opponent's costs.[2]

Clearly, it will be important to make sure that any such discussion is carefully noted on file and confirmed to the client. Failure to do so could put the firm at risk of being unable to recover its fees. Legal aid lawyers, furthermore, will need to ensure that they have ensured compliance with the Legal Services Commission's Funding Code. Broadly speaking, this was originally designed to ensure that a legally aided client should not be entitled to pursue a claim that a privately paying client of moderate means would not fund in similar circumstances.

Expertise and resources

The Guide provides sound advice on the issue of whether the work should be taken on.

> A solicitor must not act, or continue to act, where the client cannot be represented with competence or diligence.
>
> 1. This would apply where a solicitor has insufficient time, experience or skill to deal with the instructions.
> 2. Principle 12.03 will not prevent a solicitor from acting if he or she is able to do so competently by, for example, instructing counsel.
>
> The Guide, Principle 12.03 'Competence to act' and notes

Thought must be given at an early stage as to whether the firm has the time to undertake the work. For most professional advisers turning away work goes against the grain but there are obvious dangers in accepting all work to meet difficult fee earning targets. There is little point is compromising the quality of work for existing clients by taking on too much work for others. The danger is that the matter will not be dealt with expeditiously and there will be delays leading to complaints or claims. Accepting instructions where a lawyer has little or no time to act on those instructions is fraught with danger. The most common examples are agreeing to act in litigation where limitation is on the point of expiry or where there is to be a hearing in the immediate future, or in property work for a purchaser on the morning of an auction. The standard of care expected of an adviser when accepting late instructions is exactly the same as when they have time to prepare more thoroughly. The client's initial gratitude at finding an adviser can soon turn to dissatisfaction with the service provided. In some cases a lawyer with the appropriate level of experience might make a judgment that he or she will be able to take a matter on at short notice but this needs careful consideration, usually at partner level.

The lawyer undertaking the work must also have the appropriate skill levels to do the work properly. This is mostly about getting the right person to do the job. To ensure that this is done, the firm should have in place effective procedures for allocation, delegation and the subsequent supervision of work. Although the Guide envisages instructing counsel as one method of ensuring that the client receives appropriate service, great care is needed with this approach. Simply instructing counsel does not relieve the firm of its basic responsibilities to the client.

Previous experience

Lawyers should think very carefully before accepting instructions from a client who has previously complained about the firm or sued it for negligence. Sadly, the number of clients who have previously threatened or used violence against solicitors or their staff is on the increase and some thought will be needed as to the risk of such events recurring. Many will also regard the transfer of an ongoing matter to them where there is already dissatisfaction with the current advisers as being high risk under an initial risk assessment (see Lexcel, section 6.8b).

Client's expectations

The expectations of the client contain many pointers to possible later problems. Issues to address here include timescale, expectations as to costs and the likely outcome of a case. It is important that the client's expectations are addressed and, if these are unrealistic, the client needs to be told so. It is natural enough to want to establish a good and friendly relationship with the client but not at the expense of failing to provide unpalatable advice sooner rather than later. The cost–benefit analysis referred to above should be undertaken at this stage.

Reputation

Clients are becoming more sophisticated in the selection of their service suppliers and some attach considerable importance to the issue of reputation. Before the firm takes on a new client, consideration should be given as to whether any commercial conflicts could arise. If, for example, the firm acts for a high-profile animal charity, it may need to think twice about accepting instructions from a client whose activities may offend the principles of that charity. Further, certain clients have reputations that should serve as a warning. A reluctance to pay fees, a history of instructing large numbers of law firms or a reputation for being at the lower end of respectability should all serve as warnings to a firm to consider carefully whether it wants, or should act for, the client in question.

Risk assessment

It is crucial that the partners are aware of the risk exposure that will attach to the work being undertaken within the firm. In Lexcel there is a requirement that lists of the generic risks associated with areas of work that are undertaken are maintained and 'communicated to all staff' (section 6.7c). In addition, an initial risk assessment is required on every new matter by section 6.8b. This is usually achieved by requiring an assessment of the risk profile on the matter opening form as either 'normal' or 'high' risk, with a description in the office manual of those circumstances that would lead the partners to regard the matter as being out of the norm and therefore higher risk.[3] Another reason for assessing the risk in any given matter is to assist in determining what the fees should be, especially in commercial work. The greater the risk, the greater the reward should be. Figure 6.1 is a simple diagram that should be completed by inserting a tick in the appropriate box as part of the risk analysis. The completed diagram should never reveal high risk, low reward. The reverse case of low risk to high reward is, of course, much more acceptable.

It should be remembered that the analysis of risk on a matter is not a one-off consideration. It is a requirement in Lexcel at section 6.8c that any 'change to the risk profile of the matter from the client's point of view' should be reported to the appointed risk manager 'without delay'. Risk should be monitored throughout the transaction and any variance reported to the supervising partner. A transaction assessed as low risk at the outset may escalate rapidly in risk as the retainer progresses. Should this happen then it may be necessary to revise any estimate for costs and also to take steps to ensure that the fee earner has the appropriate skill, expertise and time to deal with the matter and notify the client. It is also a requirement of Lexcel that the client should be informed of any adverse costs orders made against the firm in relation to the client's matter (section 6.8d).

	Low	Medium	High
Risk			
Reward			

Figure 6.1   Risk analysis

The issues addressed above should form the major elements of a client vetting procedure but the list is not exhaustive. Many practitioners will additionally want to rely in part on the so-called 'smell test'. If the matter feels wrong, it may well be. Caution will often be the better part of valour as long as it does not simply validate discriminatory prejudice. Every firm should consider the issues that need to be addressed in their client vetting procedure, which include both generic risk issues and also issues that may be specific to the firm – taking into account its own risk profile.

Many firms or individual lawyers will consider the above points as a matter of course when taking on a client. However, as with most risk management in law firms, this might be done on an ad hoc basis. What is required is a formal process to be followed so as to ensure that all areas are addressed, considered and then acted upon. There may be opposition within the firm as the process will be viewed by some as being unduly bureaucratic. The aim should be to convince everyone concerned that the steps being taken will benefit all by avoiding later problems.

Many firms have concluded that the most effective way to carry out client vetting is by means of an IT program. This has the benefit of reducing the amount of time taken on the exercise and making the collation and retrieval of information easier. There will also be an audit trail of the checks that have been undertaken so that should a problem arise in the future and proof is needed that a conflict or money laundering check was undertaken, this can be provided. A workflow program may be developed or purchased that will address the various steps to be taken. This can also mean that much of the work may be undertaken by someone other than the lawyer, thus relieving them of the administrative burden.

EXAMPLE   **Client vetting by IT program**

Firm A, consisting of some 25 partners, implemented a client vetting system. It elected to purchase an IT package. The system identified the specific steps that had to be followed. The firm decided to use the Accounts department as the 'gateway' into the firm. It already had a system whereby the files were opened in the Accounts department and given a client/matter number, thus enabling the fee earners to start time recording and undertake financial transactions. There was a member of the Accounts staff who was responsible for carrying out this procedure. That individual's responsibilities were extended to include the new procedure. A policy decision was taken that no file would be opened without all the steps in the vetting process being completed, unless there were exceptional circumstances signed off by the head of department who accepted responsibility for the decision.

> A form was designed for electronic completion and submission by way of e-mail to the file opening team. This form addressed all the above issues, and was processed by the Accounts department; when all steps had been complied with the file was opened and an account number allocated to it. Confirmation was e-mailed to the fee earner who was then able to commence working on behalf of the client. Alternatively, if there were any further issues to be addressed then these were identified to the fee earner with a request that the matters be dealt with and further progress monitored. Non-compliances with any steps in the procedure were reported back to the department head.
>
> Initially the procedure was greeted with hostility and the fee earners complained of the delay incurred before they could start work. These delays were identified as being due mainly to the poor quality of the data supplied by the fee earners in the file opening form. A substantial majority of the forms had to be returned. As the fee earners became more familiar with the process and further training took place, the number of forms returned dropped, and the process speeded up. File numbers were being allocated without delay. The process was also identifying potential problems (mainly conflict and risk issues) much earlier than previously, thus enabling them to be managed effectively. The quality of the work also improved with a decrease in potentially awkward and difficult clients. Eventually fee earners came to regard the process as an integral part of their workload and also as being a great time saver. They got on with the legal work, while administrative matters were dealt with by the Accounts team.

The file opening form will require considerable thought if it is being created by the firm, as opposed to a ready-made package being purchased. It is likely that the firm will use a number of forms (e.g. for money laundering and conflict checks) to address some of the issues. Where these forms can be consolidated into one the process can be simplified and so made more effective. Furthermore, the IT system should be able to offer the opportunity of storing the information electronically, which would be of considerable benefit, especially with regard to the obligations for storing evidence of compliance with money laundering identification procedures.

Another real benefit of utilising an IT system is that it makes monitoring compliance and file audit procedures much easier. The system should be programmed to undertake exception reporting, so that areas of non-compliance may be readily identified and reported to the department head or other appropriate person for further investigation and, where necessary, remedial action. Some form of continual checking will be needed to ensure compliance with the process. IT will assist with the easier identification of those files where there is evidence or a suggestion of non-compliance.

An IT-based system is not essential. Smaller firms may not have the financial resources to invest in such a system and may find a manual system just as effective. The important point is that the risk issues are addressed and managed. If this involves a checklist on the file, which is manually completed and then signed off by a partner, and it is effective, then that would be satisfactory.

Collation of the above information will enable the firm to make an informed decision as to whether it is financially and commercially viable to act for the client, as well as whether it wants to act or is able to act. If the decision to proceed is made, then the information obtained will provide invaluable assistance in the next and final step in the client acquisition process – defining the retainer and recording it in writing.

Retainer letters

Confusion often arises among lawyers because of terminology in relation to what a retainer letter is and what it should do. The retainer letter is also often referred to as the engagement letter. There are no specific rules to address the points, but the following provides a guide. The retainer letter should define the contractual relationship with the client, by setting out what the firm will and will not be doing on behalf of the client. Note 1 to Principle 12.08 of the Guide provides as follows:

> A solicitor must act within his or her client's express or implied authority. It is essential at the outset for a solicitor to agree clearly with the client the scope of the retainer and subsequently to refer any matter of doubt to the client. If a solicitor limits the scope of the retainer it is good practice for the limits of the retainer to be precisely defined in writing to the client.

Some firms simply send out a pre-printed form called 'standard terms and conditions', representing the firm's terms and conditions. Relying on this document as a retainer letter is potentially risky in that each matter may vary. In the decision in *Pickersgill* v. *Riley* [2004] UKPC 14 Lord Scott stated:

> It is plain that when a solicitor is instructed in a transaction, a duty of care arises. But it is also plain that the scope of that duty is variable. It will depend first and foremost, upon the content of the instructions given to the solicitor by the client. The scope of the duty may vary depending on the characteristics of the client, in so far as they are apparent to the solicitor.

Each retainer will have to be drafted to reflect the particular case. While there will be standard matters that a firm will wish to include, such as limitation of liability, the letter should not be in pre-printed form. There is, of course, no objection to a retainer letter drafted to meet the particular requirements of a case referring to standard terms and conditions that are enclosed.

In many firms the Rule 15 letter is not the retainer letter. Also referred to as the client care letter, this document needs to address the matters that a lawyer is required to deal with in accordance with his or her professional regulations, including the Solicitors' Costs Information and Client Care Code. It is perfectly acceptable to combine the Rule 15 letter and the retainer letter and include the standard terms and conditions with that one letter. Many practitioners consider this preferable and an example of this approach can be seen in the *Lexcel Office Procedures Manual* as drafted by Tony Girling.[4]

The importance of the retainer letter must not be underestimated. In any action for professional negligence involving a lawyer, the judge will look in the first instance at the retainer letter to see what had been agreed between the lawyer and the client. The absence of such a document will make for a difficult time in defending any such action. Judicial expectations are that there will be such a letter and it is difficult to understand how a matter could proceed without this basic step having been complied with.

It is also very important to appreciate that the terms of the retainer should be kept under constant review. This is because as the matter progresses the lawyer may become aware of information or facts that cause the lawyer to review what he or she is able to do for the client and the steps that will be taken. The client might also change instructions or introduce new aspects to the transaction, which will require the retainer letter to be amended. Where this becomes necessary it should be done at the first available opportunity. Lexcel reflects these requirements at 8.6 with its provision that:

> Save in exceptional cases the client must be consulted upon and kept informed of the strategy in the matter and any planned changes to it.

Again, this procedure is likely to meet considerable resistance from lawyers, especially where speed is of the essence or is perceived to be so. Corporate lawyers tend to be the most reluctant to send retainer letters, with excuses ranging from 'the client doesn't want them' to 'we don't have time'. In all areas of work, however, the prospect of even the most amenable client later claiming that they did not agree to a course of action that was taken needs to be taken seriously. The strategy being taken for the client should always be underpinned by clear confirmation of instructions.

Letters of non-engagement

The client acquisition process may result in a decision being made not to act on behalf of a client, or alternatively the problem may arise during the retainer, which results in the firm ceasing to act in accordance with Principle 12.12 set out in the Guide dealing with termination of retainer. In such a situation it would be sensible to ensure that the client is fully aware of what has happened by sending a letter of disengagement or non-engagement.

If it does prove necessary to terminate a retainer during its existence then a disengagement letter should be sent. The objective is to ensure that the former client understands that the retainer has been terminated and that the firm is no longer representing his or her interests. The actual content of the letter will be dictated by the circumstances leading up to the termination. Core issues that should be addressed in such a letter include the reason for the termination set out in clear, easy-to-understand terminology. If the reason relates to non-payment of fees, a detailed breakdown of what has been paid and when, the sums still outstanding and copies of invoices rendered should be provided. Where there is a conflict of interest an explanation should be provided as to the impact of the professional rules. There is particular sensitivity in cases involving pending litigation and the client should be informed of the reasons for the application to come off the record and the implications of this.

Where a client simply disappears this creates a difficult situation for the solicitor. It is probably incumbent on the solicitor to make all reasonable enquiries as to the whereabouts of the client. At very least the solicitor should write to the client at his or her last known address setting out the steps taken to try to locate the client. Furthermore, the client should be advised of the implications of failing to respond to requests for information, such as limitation periods expiring, a critical date being missed and costs implications. In legally aided matters, failure to receive instructions will trigger file closing procedures and the firm should be sure to make a claim for payment within the prescribed time limits to avoid any costs penalties.

Notes

1   On the need to check on the identification of principals, see the Law Society Money Laundering Guidance at para.3.70, which refers to the need for 'reasonable measures' to be taken.
2   There are similar provisions at 2.03(4) in the draft Rule 2.
3   For an example see the *Lexcel Office Procedures Manual* at Appendix 8c, p.176.
4   Ibid, Appendix 7b at pp.146–150.

Confidentiality and conflicts of interest

Conflicts of interest and confidentiality issues are, for very good reasons, more common in legal practice than in any other professional sector. Knowing what to do for the best when problems do arise can be difficult. In a number of areas of solicitor regulation there are arguments that commercial practice needs a different set of principles from those that apply to the high street: this argument is at its most convincing in relation to conflicts. It might be readily apparent that a high street firm should not act for both parties in a divorce, but the position of a major international practice that is consulted over banking litigation when it has represented most lending institutions in recent years is distinctly more tricky. Little wonder that most of the recent developments in this field of legal practice have been inspired by the experiences and submissions of the largest commercial firms.

The difficulties faced by major firms in this area became headline business news in the summer of 2004 in relation to a possible take-over bid for Marks & Spencer by Philip Green (*Marks & Spencer Plc* v. *Freshfields Bruckhaus Deringer* [2004] EWCA Civ 741). On an application by Freshfields Bruckhaus Deringer it was held that the firm should be restrained from acting, advising or otherwise assisting in a consortium in connection with a take-over since it had previously advised the company on another matter. The judge concluded that its previous experience produced a real or serious risk of conflict of interest and that effective barriers would not be capable of being established in the firm to safeguard confidentiality.

As this case illustrated, there are few more complex issues dealt with by professional regulations than those arising in this field. Confidentiality and conflicts tend to be considered together since a conflict of interest will always produce difficulties in relation to the duty of confidentiality. A firm acting in a conflict situation will be failing to meet its duty to one client or another. Either it will be unable to represent one client as effectively as it should or the firm will be failing another client in so doing. One client or the other, or quite possibly both, could claim to have been failed in the service provided.

Confidentiality

Professional conduct rules

Not surprisingly the duty of confidentiality is one of the 'core duties' that the new draft professional conduct rules are based upon. These make the simple requirements that:

> You must keep all information about clients confidential.
>
> Draft Rule 1.04

and

> You must not act where there is a conflict between
>
> - your interests and your client's interests; or
> - the interests of two or more clients (except in strict accordance with rule 3).
>
> Draft Rule 1.05

The new draft provisions are not too dissimilar to the more familiar existing Practice Rule 1, which places solicitors under a duty to act in the best interests of the client. The Guide sees Practice Rule 1 as being so basic that all the provisions that follow are subsidiary to it. Likewise, the new draft Rule 1 is described in its guidance as forming 'over arching principles, with the other rules providing greater detail addressed to specific situations'.

The underlying duty of confidentiality will be familiar to all lawyers but is sometimes placed at risk when a firm fails to provide suitable induction training for new personnel who have not previously worked in the professional sector. Ideally there should be some introductory session on the first day for all new personnel, stressing the importance of the issue and making it clear that breaches of the duty are likely to be treated as disciplinary offences, potentially leading to instant dismissal. The *Lexcel Office Procedures Manual* contains a general notice for staff on the importance of confidentiality within its suggested procedures for client care (see section 8.16 at p.169). This reminds personnel that even so much as to reveal that the firm is instructed by a named client can, in many circumstances, amount to a breach of confidentiality and that a client's address should usually only be given out with express consent. The guidance that accompanies the new draft Solicitors' Practice (Confidentiality and Disclosure) Amendment Rule contains some other useful reminders on what can amount to a breach of confidentiality:

- the contents of a will must not be revealed during the lifetime of the testator, nor may they be after the death of the testator before probate is granted other than with the express approval of the executors;
- a lender will not usually be entitled to see a full copy of a conveyancing file without the consent of the borrower client 'unless the lender can show to your satisfaction that there is a prima facie case of fraud';
- solicitors may not factor their book debts unless the client consents since the bill is confidential.

The same guidance warns about shared office facilities and outsourced office services. Neither is prohibited but there will a responsibility for the adviser to ensure that client confidentiality is maintained.

Lexcel

There is a new provision in Lexcel dealing with confidentiality. This can be found at section 8.9c where practices are required to have documented procedures to safeguard 'the confidentiality of matter files and all other client information'. This will give rise to a range of requirements by firms and the *Lexcel Office Procedures Manual* includes consideration of such issues as leaving files in unattended cars, working on files while on the train and conducting conversations in public places on mobile telephones. There will also need to be some thought given to confidentiality issues in the reception area as a consequence of section 8.1b on client enquiries.

There is one further implication of confidentiality in the Lexcel standard. The view has always been that to open a file to an external assessor is a prima facie breach of confidentiality. This is overcome by obtaining the client's consent to inspection in the manner envisaged by the *Lexcel Assessment Guide* (see pp.13–15). For sample wording that might be added to the retainer or client care letter, see the *Lexcel Office Procedures Manual*, p.145, 'Quality standards'. At first in the Lexcel scheme the guidance stated that specific informed consent from the client was needed but the guidance now suggests that client consent can be assumed unless otherwise stated, though this position is potentially open to judicial review. The wording should state that the clients need feel under no pressure to agree to a possible inspection and that they may withhold their consent if they wish, in which case work on their file will not be affected in any way. The view of the Law Society is also that advisers may decline to consent to the disclosure of a file on an inspection if they feel that the client would or should resist this, as where there are highly personal circumstances recorded on file or price-sensitive information in commercial work. Lexcel assessors will usually simply accept a substitute file where this does arise, but could alternatively inspect the file through an intermediary. This is a particular problem in childcare work where there will be great sensitivity to much of the evidence and legal provisions prohibit disclosure of such files.

Conflicts of interest

In relation to conflicts the most obvious problems arise where a solicitor purports to act on behalf of two clients who have adverse interests. Bearing in mind that a solicitor is under a duty to act in the best interests of a client, and that the solicitor must not do anything that compromises that obligation, he or she is immediately placed in an untenable position. A common source of difficulties arises from acting for different members of the same family. Where a solicitor has acted for members of a family and then is asked to act against one or more of them, care is needed. The most common instance of this is where one party requests family law advisers to represent them in relation to the breakdown of a relationship. It has become common practice in such situations to seek the permission of the other party in the relationship to continue to act, where the firm has previously undertaken the conveyancing work for the parties together, and then decline to act if there is an objection.

Interests of former clients

It should be stressed that problems are not limited to situations involving two or more current clients. It is quite clear that there are continuing duties to former clients and this may well prohibit the firm from acting in situations that arise well after the particular retainer has expired. The fiduciary relationship with the client may end with the retainer, but the solicitor will remain in possession of confidential information, which will continue to inhibit his or her freedom to act to some degree. More worrying still is that duties could arise where no formal retainer was ever agreed in the first place.

EXAMPLE *Davies* v. *Davies* [2000] 1 FLR 39

In 1991 the wife had a 'lengthy one-off consultation' on possible divorce proceedings with a solicitor – 'T'. She issued proceedings in 1998 and found that T had accepted instructions from the husband to act on his behalf. T refused to stand down when asked to do so, pointing out that he had no recollection of the consultation and there was no evidence of the wife being unfairly prejudiced by previous events. A summons was issued to question whether T might act and it was then suggested that this matter should be dropped if all parties bore their own costs. When this was not accepted it was held that a costs order should be made against the husband since a proper application had been made. The interests of justice demanded that a solicitor with confidential information should not be seen to be risking its disclosure in any way to opposing parties.

Problems could well arise where the solicitor subsequently accepts instructions on behalf of a new client to whom the confidential information relating to the former client is relevant. When a solicitor acts on behalf of a client he or she is under a duty to disclose all relevant information in his possession relating to that client's matter. If that relevant information is confidential information relating to a former client, then to disclose it would be a breach of confidence unless the former client were to consent – hence the potential conflict. The solicitor is in an invidious position, since to disclose the information would place the solicitor in breach of the duty to protect the former client and not to disclose would mean the solicitor was failing in his or her duty to disclose fully to the new client's matter. The only sensible option is for the solicitor in this situation to withdraw. Detailed guidance on this point is to be found at Principle 15.02 of the Guide:

> If a solicitor or firm of solicitors has acquired relevant confidential information about an existing or former client during the course of acting for that client, the solicitor or the firm must not accept instructions to act against the client.

Family situations are fraught with danger for the adviser since a common interest can suddenly break down and place the family members in opposition to each other, as illustrated by the example at page 75. Even if unpleasantries have not broken out, different individuals might have developed contrary interests that should be considered independently. Interestingly, the guidance to the draft Solicitors Practice (Conflict) Amendment Rule does envisage that there may be a 'common interest' when a solicitor acts for different family members and that this will be permissible as long as any areas of conflict between them are ' "substantially less important" to all the clients than their common purpose'. It is clear that, whatever the eventual precise wording that is adopted on the issue of conflicts, continuing care is needed as such situations develop. In family situations in particular, conflicts might be obvious at the outset of some matters, but in other matters can easily develop as the matter continues, making such conflicts more difficult to identify. The solicitor needs to be alert to the risk of a conflict arising during the course of the retainer and not just at the outset.

Solicitor's interests

A further source of conflicts arises where the solicitor's personal interests conflict with those of the client. Chapter 15 of the Guide describes in some detail situations where the solicitor's interests may conflict with those of the client. While many of the situations described envisage an 'economic' conflict, such as the solicitor obtaining a personal interest or benefit in a transaction in which he or she is acting for a client, there is also reference to the fact that if a solicitor enters into a sexual relationship with a client a conflict may arise. More difficult to safeguard against is the situation where the relationship is between the client and a member of the practice's staff in areas such as crime.

Interests of two existing clients

A final source of problems is where there are conflicts between two existing clients. It has been accepted practice in crime for many years for an adviser to represent co-accused until a dispute breaks out between them – perhaps each claims that the other was the ringleader and that they were very much a secondary party. It was this situation that prompted a dispute between the Law Society and the legal aid authorities when the Society's new draft conflict rules were unveiled in 2004 providing that:

> If you are required to do anything on behalf of one co-defendant which will undermine the position of any of the others you must cease to act for one and possibly all.[1]

Whatever the type of conflict, consideration of the issue will need to form part of the client vetting procedure. When accepting instructions it is for the solicitor to prove that there was no reasonable prospect of a conflict between two clients. Arguments that the onus is on the complainant to prove a conflict were dismissed in *Re A Firm of Solicitors* [1995] 3 All ER 482.

Lexcel and professional rules

The Lexcel standard deals with conflicts of interest at section 8.3 and merely provides that firms must settle their arrangements for checking up on the issue. The Lexcel guidance envisages that larger firms will need more complex checking but that smaller firms may well deal with the issue perfectly well by simpler procedures. Nor, of course, are conflicts a problem for every type of practice. A specialist immigration practice will know, for example, that it will not act for the Home Office and that conflicts will not therefore arise. The new draft professional rules do seem to assume, however, that larger firms will have more advanced conflict checking systems in place. The system used by a number of firms sending out an e-mail to all staff saying: 'The corporate department has been instructed by ABC Ltd in the acquisition XYZ Ltd. Is anyone aware of any reason as to why we should not act?' has caused problems in a number of cases. The system is too reliant on everyone opening the e-mail, reading it properly and then responding to it. Such a system should be confined to smaller practices or used as a backup to more formal checks only.

What of the situation where checking does highlight a problem? The new draft professional rules in part reflect increasing dissatisfaction with the existing rules on conflicts in recent years. Notwithstanding Law Society guidance on the topic it was apparent that many solicitors had problems in identifying a conflict and there was great scope for confusion in many cases. This was confirmed by the number of claims and complaints that were founded on conflict. There were often other pressures on solicitors to attempt to justify why they should act notwithstanding the apparent presence of a conflict, or the risk of such a conflict arising in the course of the retainer, usually the reluctance of a solicitor to forgo potentially lucrative fees and also running the risk of losing an established client. Telling an important and valued client that they have to obtain separate and independent advice from another firm is bound to seem tantamount to giving the work away and compromising the future relationship. The belief lingers that once a client has used another firm they might never return. Cutting corners on this issue is understandable but can rebound with the most unpleasant of consequences.

Chinese walls

There has been a good deal of debate and litigation in recent years as to whether solicitors can validly deal with conflict situations by erecting so-called Chinese walls. This will involve getting another fee earner – preferably in another office – to deal with the matter. The better view is that such arrangements might be an expedient for safeguarding confidentiality but they are unlikely to overcome a conflict. The leading case of *His Royal Highness Prince Jefri Bolkiah* v. *KPMG* [1999] 2 WLR 215 fell short of ruling that Chinese walls (or 'information barriers' as they are more commonly now referred to) would be ineffective in every case. On the other hand this influential House of Lords decision made it quite clear that the courts would need some convincing that an information barrier erected by a professional adviser was in fact effective. Notwithstanding this ruling there developed a misplaced belief among many solicitors that in order to have an effective wall it was sufficient simply to instruct another lawyer in a different part of the building or in another office. This was not the case and there were many commentators who expressed doubts as to whether information barriers could ever be effective. To stand any chance at all there would have to be physical barriers in place in the firm, for example by use of different offices, and the number of staff involved should be relatively few. This was presumably based on the assumption that the more staff there were involved in a transaction, the greater would be the chance of information being leaked. The likelihood of inadvertent disclosure, as from firm-wide computerised information systems, was often seen as being as much of a risk as more deliberate communication by those concerned in the transaction.

Further concerns grew in relation to the recruitment of new personnel by practices. In *Halewood International Ltd* v. *Addleshaw Booth & Co* [2000] Lloyd's Rep PN 298 the firm recruited a solicitor – 'R' – who had previously acted for the claimant in relation to a dispute on 'Lambrini' drinks. Later, Addleshaw Booth & Co accepted instructions for Italian wine growers in relation to the similar 'Lambrusco' drink. Although R was not personally involved in this new matter, the claimant sought an injunction to restrain the firm from acting, on grounds that R might pass on confidential information about its commercial operations. It was held that it was appropriate that R should be based in a different office of the firm while the litigation continued – the claimant accepting an undertaking to this effect.

Potentially this line of argument could have conflicted most major firms out of most litigation work, but a more common-sense line on the issue of partners and staff recruitment was established by the later case of *Koch Shipping Inc* v. *Richards Butler* [2002] EWCA Civ 1280. In this case an injunction was held not to be justified where the defendant's former solicitor – 'P' – obtained a position at the claimant firm. The court held that the correct approach was as outlined in the *Prince Jefri* case – was there a 'real risk' of disclosure? It also commented, however, that all such decisions would hinge on their particular facts and that these would be 'infinitely variable'. The major factors in this case included that it was only one individual who had the confidential information; that she was of unquestioned integrity and fully understood her duties of confidentiality; and also that there were physical barriers between her and those dealing with the matter. The solicitor, P, had also given undertakings not to have dealings with the team in question. The court suggested that a 'robust view' should be taken in such cases and that the risk of breach of confidentiality in such cases would often be 'fanciful or theoretical'.

Need for change

One of the things that became increasingly apparent from all such cases was that the conflict guidance was failing to meet the demands of the modern-day corporate environment in which leading commercial firms now operate. These firms have a multi-jurisdictional presence and in the main act for clients of similar standing. Situations often arose where the firm was asked to act on behalf a client but could not do so as it would be in breach of the guidance. The instructions then had to be declined. Even more questionable, this might be the case even though both clients involved in the potential conflict had no objection to the firm acting. The guidance did seem more suited to the smaller high street or rural practice and ran the risk of preventing larger practices from undertaking work on behalf of sophisticated clients with full knowledge of the material facts. Such clients are attracted to firms that are noted for their expertise in a sector such as banking work and yet that very experience could debar a firm from acting. Nor was it simply the firms that were becoming exasperated at being put to the inconvenience of turning away work – clients also had to go the inconvenience of seeking out alternative sources of advice.

Change was needed and the Law Society recognised this. This need for change has resulted in the drafting of new rules relating to conflict of interest and confidentiality and disclosure. At the time of publication these rules have been approved by the Council of the Law Society and await Schedule 4 approval (this being the approval of the Department of Constitutional Affairs and the Master of the Rolls). There has been a delay in that the proposals relating to criminal lawyers and the restriction on acting for more than one defendant in a trial have caused some consternation within the Legal Services Commission. If these late differences can be resolved the rules should be approved in substantially the same form as the drafts. It is envisaged that they will eventually become Rules 3 and 4 in the new regulatory framework.

The proposed new rules on conflicts arise from difficulties of unduly restrictive and vague regulations. A new rule has also been introduced to deal with conflicts between the duties of confidentiality, disclosure and information barriers. These new rules and accompanying guidance are to be welcomed and it is envisaged that they will form part of the new professional rules now being considered by the Law Society.

Solicitors' Practice (Conflict) Amendment Rule

Acting in situations of conflict of interest continues to be prohibited. The most striking change is that this Rule (which will amend Rule 16 of the Solicitors Practice Rules 1990 by making a new Rule 16D) defines conflict as being between the interests of two or more clients in relation to the *same* or *related* matters, or where the interests of the client are in conflict with those of the solicitor. The Rule goes on to state that a related matter will always include any other matter that involves the same asset or liability. The guidance states that there must be 'some reasonable degree of relationship for a conflict to arise'. It will be for the solicitor to assess if two matters are related.

Exceptions

Another important new element is that while the Rule states that a solicitor must not act if there is a conflict of interests, a number of exceptions are set out in the Rule. A firm may only act in the defined circumstances provided that the client has given its consent. There are two situations, both of which are defined. These arise when there is a 'common interest' and where there are what the guidance calls 'specialised areas of legal services where the clients are sophisticated users'. Caution must be exercised before acting for clients in these excepted circumstances. They should not be used as an excuse by the solicitor to act by adapting the facts to fit the exception.

An example of common interest given in the guidance relates to acting for several members of the same family to achieve a common purpose where all members of the family are in clear agreement as to what they wish to achieve. The 'common interest' element must not be overlooked, however. As soon as that is no longer present then there is potentially a conflict and the solicitor should withdraw, thus emphasising the need for the solicitor to assess carefully the risk of a conflict arising during the course of the retainer. The guidance also envisages the possibility of using a 'limited retainer' where there is a conflict. The objective is that the solicitor would advise on those areas where there is no conflict, and direct the clients to other advisers in relation to the conflict areas. While the logic behind this is clear, in practice it may be very difficult to remain within the parameters of a defined retainer. Clients might also be unhappy and suspicious about having to consult separate solicitors in relation to one aspect of a transaction.

Sophisticated users of specialised legal services are often frustrated by the fact that they are unable to instruct the lawyer of their choice by reason of the existing conflict principles. They may need recourse to specialist legal advice that is only available from a limited number of lawyers with the relevant expertise in a niche area. These sophisticated users will be perfectly capable of making an informed decision as to whether or not they are happy to instruct a lawyer in a potential conflict situation. The degree of cost and aggravation in trying to find another lawyer may out-weigh the conflict risk. Furthermore, sophisticated users will often have their own in-house legal advisers to help them reach a decision and the new Rule 16D has been drafted to reflect this fact. For a solicitor to be able to act notwithstanding a potential conflict, the following conditions of new Rule 16D will need to be met:

1. The clients are competing for the same asset, which if obtained by one client, will make it unobtainable to the other.
2. There is no other conflict or significant risk of a conflict arising.
3. The clients have given their informed consent in writing, all relevant facts pertaining to the conflict having been disclosed.
4. Unless the client consents, no one solicitor acts for or supervises more than one of the client's affairs.

Further requirements include telling the client clearly so that he or she understands all the relevant issues relating to the conflict, that the solicitor is satisfied that the client understands all the issues, and that the client is of full capacity. It is stressed that there are *no* excepted circumstances where a solicitor may act when the solicitor's interests conflict with those of the client.

Solicitors' Practice (Confidentiality and Disclosure) Amendment Rule

This Rule deals with the conflict that may arise between the solicitor's duty of confidentiality and disclosure, which has been explained in more detail above, as well as the establishment of information barriers. It will amend Rule 16 of the Solicitors Practice Rules 1990 and is numbered Rule 16E.

The duty of confidentiality and disclosure is detailed in the Rule, as is the duty not to put confidentiality at risk by acting. As with the proposed Rule 16D, there are some excepted circumstances where it is permissible for a solicitor to act in a situation that would otherwise be prohibited.

It is made clear that the duty of confidentiality extends beyond the termination of the retainer. This emphasises the need to keep accurate records of which clients the firm has acted for and in what context, as it may become important to access an archived file to ascertain whether or not the firm is in possession of confidential information. The guidance to the Rule highlights the fact that information received in the context of a joint retainer must be made available between the clients and that a sol-icitor may obtain information that is deemed confidential in respect of an individual, even though that individual does not subsequently instruct the firm. Again, this emphasises the need to ensure that all information received or advice given to an individual is recorded, irrespective of whether they go on to become a client of the firm as in the *Davies* case above. The information must be available for the purpose of a conflict search at later date.

Exceptions

The exceptions to the duty not to put confidentiality at risk are subject to obtaining the consent of both clients concerned. The further conditions that need to be met for a solicitor to be able to act are as follows:

1. The client needs to be aware that the practice holds confidential information that cannot be disclosed to the client.
2. The solicitor must have a reasonable belief that both clients understand the issues.
3. Both clients must agree to the conditions under which the solicitor will act.
4. It is reasonable in the circumstances to do so.

There is also provision in the Rule for the situation where a solicitor has been acting for both clients and a conflict problem arises. In such a case the solicitor may continue to act for one client if they have the clear consent of the other.

The exceptions to the duty not to put confidentiality at risk are extended to cover the situation where neither client's consent has been obtained. This exception allows a solicitor to act for a client on an otherwise prohibited matter without the consent of the client, or former client, in respect of whom confidential information is held provided:

1. It is not possible to obtain the informed consent from the client or former client.
2. The solicitor's client has agreed to the solicitor acting, notwithstanding that the solicitor or the firm holds confidential information that cannot be disclosed.
3. Safeguards that comply with the standards required by law are put in place.
4. It is reasonable in all the circumstances to do so.

What is or is not reasonable is not defined, and so might be open to challenge. The obvious advice must be to proceed with considerable caution in such a situation.

Information barriers

Rule 16E is not specific on the steps that are necessary in order to create an information barrier. The guidance, however, does go into some detail on this. It sets out what a firm may have to do in order to satisfy the Rule and comply with the standards required by law. It is quite clear that simply getting a fee earner in another office to act is not a sufficient information barrier.

The guidance envisages two situations: where the client has consented and where they have not. In the former situation it is stated that it is for the solicitor or firm to agree the safeguards, but it would normally be necessary to satisfy points (a) to (f) below, with some of (g) to (m) also being applicable. In the latter situation the firm must satisfy the requirements of common law and most if not all of the points (a) to (n) listed below.

These points are:

(a) that the client who or which might be interested in the confidential information acknowledges in writing that the information held by the firm will not be given to them;

(b) that all members of the firm who hold the relevant confidential information ('the restricted group') are identified and have no involvement with or for the other client;

(c) that no member of the restricted group is managed or supervised in relation to that matter by someone from outside of the restricted group;

(d) that all members of the restricted group confirm at the start of the engagement that they understand that they possess or might come to possess information which is confidential, and that they must not discuss it with any other member of the firm unless that person is, or becomes a member of the restricted group, and that this obligation shall be regarded by everyone as an on-going one;

(e) that each member of the restricted group confirms when the barrier is established that they have not done anything which would amount to a breach of the information barrier; and

(f) that only members of the restricted group have access to documents containing the confidential information.

The following arrangements may also be appropriate, and might in particular be necessary where a solicitor is acting without consent:

(g) that the restricted group is physically separated from those acting for the other client, for example, by being in a separate building, on a separate floor or in a segregated part of the offices, and that some form of 'access restriction' be put in place to ensure physical segregation;

(h) that confidential information on computer systems is protected by use of separate computer networks or through use of password protection or similar means;

(i) that the firm issues a statement that it will treat any inadvertent breach of the information barrier as a serious disciplinary offence;

(j) that each member of the restricted group gives a written statement at the start of the engagement that they understand the terms of the information barrier and will comply with them;

(k) that the firm undertakes that it will do nothing which would or might prevent or hinder any member of the restricted group from complying with the information barrier;

(l) that the firm identifies a specific partner or other appropriate person within the 'restricted group' with overall responsibility for the information barrier;

(m) that the firm provides formal and regular training for members of the firm on duties of confidentiality and responsibility under information barriers or will ensure that such training is provided prior to the engagement being undertaken; and

(n) that the firm implements a system for the opening of post, receipt of faxes and distribution of email which will ensure that confidential information is not disclosed to anyone outside the restricted group.

The draft rules have received a welcome from most observers since they not only provide clarity, but make the job of the solicitor easier by defining conflict and confidentiality. Setting out the steps that may be required of a solicitor to erect an effective barrier will be particularly helpful in commercial practice.

Conflict checks

The draft rules also underline the importance of a firm undertaking an effective conflict of interest check at the outset of the retainer. A conflict check system is only as effective as the quality of the information that is available to be searched against to identify any potential conflicts. The conflicts check must go beyond simply looking to see if the firm has acted for the client before. Conflicts and confidentiality issues can arise in other situations.

EXAMPLE   **Identity of client**

A firm offers legal services across a variety of legal disciplines. These include corporate services and matrimonial services. The matrimonial department accepts instructions, only to discover that the spouse of their client is a director of a major corporate client. This only comes to light when the director receives a letter from the firm itemising his misdemeanours and making the financial implications of those misdemeanours clear. Had the director's name, not just the name of the company, been inserted on the conflict database the potential conflict and confidentiality issues would have been identified beforehand. This would have avoided the loss of an important client for the corporate department and also the added embarrassment of having to tell the wife that the firm would not be able to act for her owing to the potential conflict and/or disclosure issue.

There are many IT-based systems available for conflict checking. Some firms have tied the conflict check into the client vetting procedure and mechanised the whole process, which is to be recommended. Another important feature of the procedure as mentioned above is to collate the relevant information to enable an effective search to be carried out.

Depending on the potential for conflict problems, firms should consider preparing a conflict check form like the one in Box 7.1 for use by fee earners. This will require the fee earner to obtain relevant information from a potential client as early in the relationship as possible.

In summary, it is for the firm to decide upon the format of the conflict checks that it needs. Much will depend on the nature of the firm, although many of the basic elements identified in the form at Figure 7.1 should be included. In most cases a conflict check should be carried out on every new matter, even if the solicitor is acting for an existing client who is well known to the firm. The solicitor must also be alive to conflicts arising in the course of a retainer and it may be necessary to undertake further conflict checks as the matter progresses. Such instances arise where another party is joined in to an action in a litigation matter or if it is decided that the purchase of a commercial property will proceed in the name of an alternative subsidiary company. Any such situation will result in new parties being part of the matter and they will need to be cleared for conflict or confidentiality issues.

Firms that operate in alternative jurisdictions must also be aware of any conflict issues that may arise in that particular jurisdiction. It is recommended that firms build into their database details of organisations that should be avoided because of national or international embargo provisions. It is illegal to export certain goods to certain countries and solicitors should be careful not to become involved by reason of default in such illegal activities. Although not strictly a conflict issue, these are matters that can most effectively be addressed at the conflict check stage by ensuring that the information is stored on the conflict database.

BOX 7.1   **Conflict check form**

Fee earner
Office
Department

Supervising partner
Other team members

Client full names
Associates (i.e. subsidiary companies)
Additional names (directors, major shareholders)

Adverse parties (other side in litigation; seller of property if acting for buyer)
Associates
Additional names

Is the client an existing client?
Industry sector?

Additional relevant information

Note

1   Quote taken from para.21 of the Conflict Guidance (explanatory notes to Rule 16D) July 2004 version. For details of objections of the LSC to this, see [2004] *Gazette*, 16 September, 1.

Progressing matters

- Progress and costs
- Undertakings
- Counsel and experts
- Risk reviews
- Checklists

One of the more obvious improvements that can be made in many firms is in regard to basic levels of file maintenance. If papers cannot be found, or are overlooked because of misfiling, mistakes are very much more likely to happen. When legally sensitive materials cannot be found the client's position may be compromised. If litigation involves the wrong evidence, because similar items from other matters have been confused with the correct items, the implications for all concerned could be severe. It follows that the prospects of a matter being well processed are greatly enhanced if file management techniques promote efficiency of operations throughout the firm.

Section 8.9 of the Lexcel standard provides that firms should be able to identify all matters and, where appropriate, the particular funders behind them. A firm must, for example, be able to identify all legal aid matters and is obliged to do so under the SQM 2002, section E1.1. Problems can arise from general or miscellaneous files if these are used to circumvent normal file opening procedures. It does, however, remain standard practice in areas such as commercial work to maintain such files where regular clients will often want some minor one-off advice. As long as the files are properly controlled and any advice given can later be found and retrieved before normal file destruction periods expire there should be little to worry about. The principle of 'traceability', which appears at section 8.9b needs to extend to other items that cannot or should not be stored on the matter file. We will examine principles on wills and deeds storage in Chapter 10 on file closure.

So far as progressing matters is concerned, most firms have adapted to the requirements of professional rules in relation to the information to be confirmed to the client at the outset of a matter. There may be limitations to how this is done on any given file, but it is likely that a system will exist that broadly meets the main Law Society requirements. Where firms are more likely to be exposed to complaints and possible losses is in relation to maintaining progress once the matter is under way. All too often a complaint to the Consumer Complaints Service will involve a matter that has started with a flurry of activity, but several months later things have gone quiet. At that stage an interim bill is sent out with no accompanying explanation. The client questions why they are expected to pay when there is precious little evidence of any progress. Many firms are too quick to see this as a client not wanting to pay a bill. All too often the problem is in fact a failure by the adviser to maintain momentum, compounded by poor communication with the client.

It should also be stressed that avoiding delay in handling a client's instructions makes good business sense. In areas such as personal injury work, where the effect of conditional fee agreements is to substantially increase normal levels of work in progress and thus balance sheet value, the speedy turnaround of work becomes vital if the firm is to avoid liquidity or cash-flow problems. This has a bearing on the numbers of live files that fee earners should be expected to manage. Figure 8.1 shows an appropriate calculation by Andrew Otterburn, who has advised numerous firms and also many of the professional bodies on such issues.

Whatever the precise calculation where it can be undertaken, more partners need to understand that simply adding more work and more files to already busy fee earners will not necessarily improve financial per-

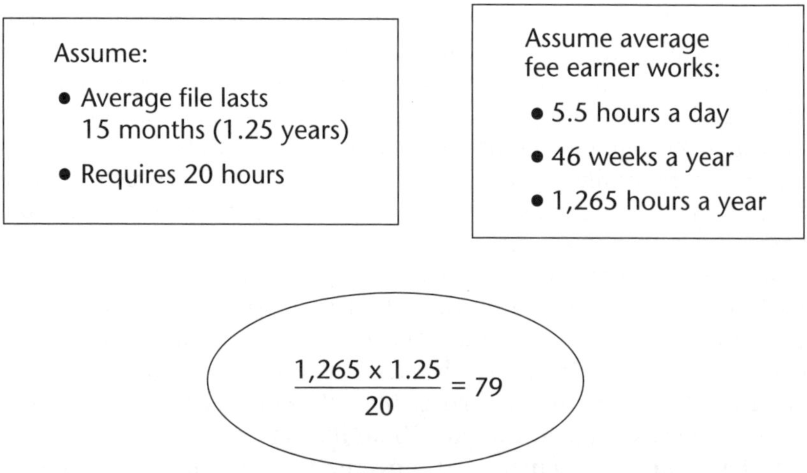

Assume:

- Average file lasts
  15 months (1.25 years)

- Requires 20 hours

Assume average
fee earner works:

- 5.5 hours a day

- 46 weeks a year

- 1,265 hours a year

$$\frac{1,265 \times 1.25}{20} = 79$$

Figure 8.1   Personal injury: example calculation of hours

formance. In many cases the opposite might be achieved by slowing down the turnover of matters. Knowing when to turn away work is increasingly a key management skill.

Progress and costs

Not surprisingly, Lexcel places a good deal of emphasis on maintaining progress in matters. The principal provisions on this are to be found at section 8.7, which provides that:

> Practices will have documented procedures to ensure that matters are progressed in an appropriate manner. In particular:
>
> a: Key information must be recorded on the file.
> b: Key dates must be recorded on the file and in a back-up system.
> c: A timely response is made to telephone calls and correspondence from the client and others.
> d: Information on cost is provided at least every six months and, in publicly funded matters, the effect of the statutory charge, if any, is provided to the client in accordance with the Solicitors' Costs Information and Client Care Code.
> e: Clients are informed in writing if the person with conduct of their matter changes, or there is a change of person to whom any problem with service should be addressed.

The effect of these provisions is to make failure to maintain and record progress a potential non-compliance with the standard. Many firms have adopted some form of frontsheet or summary form at the start of the file that enables colleagues to see the state of the matter without having to check the file more fully. This would be an appropriate standard for the great majority of files that are not too lengthy or complex. For substantial litigation or commercial files it is increasingly seen as good practice to have some central summary record that team members can consult. A good standard to set is that all files should be intelligible to others in the firm on the basis of what is on that file.

The significance of key dates systems has been referred to in Chapter 3. In Lexcel there are requirements that '[k]ey dates must be recorded in the file and in a back-up system' (section 8.7b). In practice there can be different backup arrangements within the same firm, depending in part on the work type. Litigation generates so many key or critical dates that computerised systems are likely to be advantageous. Private client work, by contrast, generates fewer dates and a well-maintained hard copy future diary is often encountered. Whatever the system employed, the department or team will need to define what they mean by 'key dates' and ensure that the mechanism for entering them on to the system is clearly established and understood. The definition suggested by the *Lexcel Office Procedures Manual* is 'any date, the missing of which could give rise to a cause of action in negligence' (section 8.11 at p.166). There then needs to be clear responsibility for monitoring the entries and alerting matter handlers of dates as they arise. Dates such as limitation periods need 'countdown dates' by way of advance notice – three months and one month are common choices. A common failure is not then to insist on a reply acknowledging receipt of the alert and confirming that action has been taken. The bitter experiences of the Solicitors Indemnity Fund resulted in a recommendation in the self-assessment questionnaire of 2000 that amendments should never be made in correction fluid – the main data should be changed and clearly initialled.

The main aim of Lexcel was to reinforce the provisions of the Solicitors' Costs Information and Client Care Code. Although the standard highlights the need for six-monthly costs updates these are only necessary under the Code 'unless otherwise agreed' (para.6(a)). The more important provision is that requiring the firm to: 'inform the client in writing as soon as it appears that a costs estimate or agreed upper limit may or will be exceeded' (para.6(c)). This latter provision has been enforced quite stringently in a number of recent cases against firms seeking costs from clients. Although originally intended more as matters of good practice than contractual rights, the costs courts have increasingly taken the view that rules of the professional body acting as regulator should be enforced in individual cases. In *Wong* v. *Vizards (A Firm)* [1997] 2 Costs LR 46 the client questioned the right of the firm to charge well in excess of an original estimate provided at the outset. An allowance of a 15 per cent margin of error was suggested by the judge. On the general principle he commented that:

> Mr Wong has just cause for complaint if, after seeking a reliable estimate from his solicitors as to his potential costs exposure before deciding to take the matter to trial, he should then be required to pay a far greater amount without further warning or a proper explanation.

This decision emphasised the obligation that clearly exists under the Code to vary estimates if necessary: 'Solicitors should not exceed an agreed limit without first obtaining the client's consent' (para.6(d)).

In *Islington & Shoreditch Housing Association* v. *Beachcroft Wansbroughs* (2002, unreported[1]) Costs Judge Wright referred to the obligation to keep costs information up to date as being 'not just a professional rule, it is a statutory requirement'. He also issued a cautionary note that this provision was 'a much thumbed part of my books because it does come up so often'. In that case the firm had provided guidance to the client that it might incur some £10,000 of costs in taking a matter to trial. In fact it exceeded this figure well before trial and continued to perform further work and invoice for it – all such interim bills being duly paid by the client. The final bill on the resolution of the matter would have taken the fees to some £25,000 but at this stage the client objected and pointed out that it had only ever been supplied with guidance that the costs figure would be some £10,000. Notwithstanding the payment of the interim invoices it was held that the amounts paid over the guide figure of £10,000 should be repaid. The firm had failed to notify the client that a costs estimate would be exceeded and was thus not entitled to be paid the amounts claimed.

This decision seems harsh to the adviser, given the communication provided by way of interim invoices. A further concern is that it may be one thing to apply this rule in litigation where matters develop relatively predictably if not slowly, but it could cause greater difficulties in corporate negotiations where a team of advisers might put in very considerable hours over a weekend if encountering a late and unexpected problem. In the early hours of the morning with the possible loss of the deal on everyone's mind it may well be that revising a previous estimate might be far from everyone's thoughts. The professional rules are not limited to long-running litigation, however, and need to be considered by practitioners of all disciplines.

Whatever the difficulties of any given situation, a system for noting estimates and alerting fee earners that the estimates are being approached should be favoured. A monthly print-out check will assist but this may be inadequate if a good deal of activity has occurred in the previous month. Case management systems that can be set to provide timely alerts have obvious advantages. Whatever the system adopted, there is little point in doing fee earning work that the firm will not get paid for.

Undertakings

The risks implicit in undertakings are well known by most. Less well known is that liability for an undertaking can arise in the course of a solicitor's private life. *The Guide to the Professional Conduct of Solicitors 1999* (the Guide) defines an undertaking as:

> any unequivocal declaration of intention addressed to someone who reasonably places reliance on it and made by:
>
> (a) a solicitor or a member of a solicitor's staff in the course of practice; or
> (b) a solicitor as 'solicitor', but not in the course of practice
>
> The Guide, Principle 18.01

The word 'undertaking' need not be used and there is no rule that oral undertakings are in any way less valid than written ones, though they may be more difficult to prove. Firms would be well advised not to accept undertakings by e-mail since it is generally impossible to prove the authorship of any message. Failure to honour an undertaking is prima facie unprofessional conduct, which can therefore be punished by the Disciplinary Tribunal. The courts also can enforce undertakings as if they were contractual debts under their inherent jurisdiction (see the Guide, Principle 18.16). Within the new draft rules failure to honour undertakings is treated as a failure of the first core duty to act with 'integrity towards clients, the courts, lawyers and others' (Rule 1.01).

There have been significant problems for firms arising from failure to handle undertakings in a satisfactory manner, most of which stem from giving undertakings that were unwise in the first place or then forgetting about them.

EXAMPLE   **Failure to review terms of undertaking**

Firm ABC acted for Mr A in his divorce. At an early stage it was agreed that the matrimonial home would be sold, with ABC having care and conduct. ABC obtained a redemption figure of some £120,000 in respect of the mortgage from the bank. The property was worth £400,000. After payment of the mortgage ABC was to account to the wife's solicitors for £200,000, being her agreed share of the capital. It undertook to do this on completion of the sale. There then followed a substantial delay before the property was sold. ABC did not bother to obtain another redemption statement until after exchange of contracts, notwithstanding that the one in its possession was then nearly five months old. The client assured the firm that he had been paying the mortgage. Unfortunately the mortgage was an all monies due certificate to the bank and had also secured business borrowing of the husband. The husband had allowed the business to get into serious financial difficulty and the bank demanded repayment of the outstanding loans. When the redemption figure arrived two days before completion, the amount required to redeem the mortgage was £305,000. The wife's solicitors enforced the undertaking.

EXAMPLE   **Failure to obtain client's authority to undertaking**

XYZ undertook to meet the lessor's solicitors' legal costs in relation to the acquisition of leasehold premises in the City of London. No upper limit was agreed and the client's irrevocable authority was not obtained to give an open undertaking. The matter dragged on for nearly 10 months, when the landlord suddenly withdrew and proceeded with another party, which was prepared to pay a higher rental. The landlord's solicitors sent in their bill of costs for £18,000. XYZ's client refused to pay it saying they would never have agreed to pay such a large sum, especially with the matter not proceeding. The landlord's solicitors enforced the undertaking.

Recognising such dangers, Lexcel has a requirement that the firms should have procedures for the 'giving, monitoring and discharge of undertakings' (section 8.8). There are very similar provisions for legal aid firms in the SQM 2002, section E1.2(d). The most sensible arrangements will usually make a distinction between the routine undertakings that are most commonly associated with conveyancing, such as to hold deeds to order or to use purchase proceeds to discharge all mortgages before accounting to the client, from the non-routine. The more unusual undertakings are probably the more dangerous for most – a common example being to account for costs to date on a long-running file when it is transferred to the firm. The norm would be to require partner authorisation for non-routine undertakings and, just as important, for confirmation of their discharge. A register of undertakings used to be insisted upon by the legal aid authorities and is found helpful by some firms, but not all. A more practical safeguard may well be to place a prominent sticker on the file with partner initials for authorisation and discharge.

Counsel and experts

The input of other advisers that the firm might involve on the client's behalf can have a very obvious bearing on the outcome of the matter for that client. It follows that the firm should exert proper control over its choice of and instructions to counsel and others. The firm could breach its anti-discrimination policy if it chooses outside advisers on grounds of gender, race or otherwise; it is a requirement of both the Law Society model policy on anti-discrimination and Lexcel that clear arrangements exist to ensure to appropriate selection criteria are employed.

Beyond this, the main requirements in Lexcel are that clients are consulted on the decision to seek outside help and also on the choice of adviser and that records are maintained on those selected for use. Potentially the most useful list is of *non*-approved advisers, but the combined effect of the rights of data subjects and the law of defamation makes the creation of such a list inadvisable. Files should show a note of clear instructions given and a careful consideration of advice when received. The requirement at Lexcel section 8.10h on payment of fees relates in part to legal aid payment arrangements but should also record the firm's commitment to treat counsel fairly. The Bar finds itself in a very odd situation by the standards of most businesses. It is dependent for all but a tiny fraction of its work on the solicitors who are increasingly its opposition. The Bar Council operates a system of listing firms that should not be provided with services where there is abuse in relation to non-payment of fees but it is understandably difficult to invoke.

Risk reviews

The risk profile of individual matters can change at any stage and it is important that the risk profile is kept under review. New developments in law or the evidence that is provided can make a reassessment of the client's position important. These will be issues for file reviews but there are also provisions requiring ongoing risk reviews at section 6.8c–d in Lexcel. During the matter the firm is obliged to:

> c: Consider any change to the risk profile of the matter from the client's point of view and report and advise on such circumstances without delay, informing the risk manager if appropriate.
> d: Inform the client in all cases where an adverse costs order is made against the firm in relation to the matter in question.

The most common risk is that the client's instructions are no longer feasible or the matter could no longer be seen as being cost-effective. In the Solicitors' Costs Information and Client Care Code this is dealt with at para.6(b), which provides that the client should have explained to them:

> any changed circumstances which will, or which are likely to affect the amount of costs, the degree of risk involved or the cost-benefit to the client of continuing with the matter; . . .

Failure to identify and advise the client on such situations should be seen to be putting the firm at the same risk of not being able to recover its costs as failure to update estimates. If the change in risk profile needs to be reported to the insurers firms have to be confident that fee earners are reporting their concerns as soon as possible.

Checklists

Finally, the following checklists of the most common risk points might be helpful in addressing changes to the risk profile of matters and in compiling the lists of 'generic risks' required by section 6.7d in Lexcel. It should be stressed that the lists below are not exhaustive, nor could they ever be, as the causes of solicitor negligence continue to grow with new legislation and decisions of the courts. It is for the department or team to prepare their own list of risks. A discussion at a departmental meeting would be a good place to start. The first two lists for property transactions are included as illustrations of how all lists adopted by the firm might eventually look. The others are lists of common pitfalls.

CHECKLIST   **Leasehold checklist**

- Obtain a copy of the lease
  - Is it complete
  - Where is the original
- Lease/sublease
  - Has the title been made available
  - Read the title
- Read all the lease
  - Does it make sense
  - Do you understand all the terms
  - Check date and commencement dates
  - Has lease been signed and stamped
- Check the unexpired term
  - Does it satisfy Council of Mortgage Lenders (CML) handbook requirements
  - Does it satisfy client's requirements
- Check the property description
  - Is it correct
  - Does it correspond with the plan
  - Has the plan been correctly coloured
- Check all of the building has been demised
- Pay special attention to garages, parking spaces
  - Are they included in the demise
  - Is it merely a right to use in common with others
- Rights
  - What rights exist in favour of the tenant
  - Is it possible to get to and from the property
  - What restrictions are there in respect of such rights
  - Hours of use
  - Payments required
  - What informal rights are enjoyed, if any
  - Are there rights of entry on to adjoining properties
- Exceptions and reservations
  - What such matters affect the property
  - In whose favour are they
  - Are there rights of entry on to the property
- Ground rent
  - Is it fixed or subject to review
  - If the latter, does the review procedure work? Check by doing a calculation. Ascertain future liability
  - Is there a need to refer for expert advice
  - Is a receipt available
  - Who collects the rent
- Are there any unusual clauses in the lease (i.e. shared ownership lease)
  - If so, and they are not clear, ask

- – Make sure you understand, otherwise you will not be able to explain to the client
- Is the lease effective/defective
  - – Lack of mutually enforceable repairing covenants, the old chestnut
  - – Deed of variation – does it work
  - – Title insurance
  - – Is it really defective
- Service charge
  - – How much, and how often is it paid
  - – To whom
  - – Accounts available, do they make sense
  - – Any large or substantial sums likely to become due
  - – Lifts
  - – Receipt
  - – External decoration
- Management company
  - – Does it exist, do a company search
  - – Obligations to the company
  - – Is it residents or professional
  - – Payments for supply of information, authorised by lease
  - – Be careful of CML requirements
- Forfeiture provisions
  - – What are they
  - – Bankruptcy – invariably unacceptable
- Insurance provisions
  - – What are they
  - – Obtain a copy of the policy and up-to-date schedule
  - – Check policy is valid
  - – Read the policy
  - – Check sums insured
  - – Consider need to refer to expert
  - – Are insurance provisions acceptable to client and lender
- Covenants and regulations
  - – Identify them
  - – In respect of regulations, have any new regulations been made
  - – Particular areas to look out for
    - – Pets
    - – Restrictions on use
    - – Alienation clauses
    - – Parking
    - – Alterations, internal/external
    - – Use of common parts, refuse/drying areas
  - – Make sure the client is advised of them
- Repairing obligations
  - – Who is responsible for repairs
  - – Who pays for repairs
  - – Can access for repairs be obtained with/without consent
- Drafting leases

- – Beware the word processor
- – Check draft with client
- – Clear accurate plan, properly coloured
- – Are client's instructions incorporated in the draft
- – Check all loose ends dealt with (incorporation of management company, etc.)

Always, always remember CML handbook requirements. The mortgage lender is a client as well. Particular care should be paid in respect of the following:
- Term
- Maintenance companies
- Ground rent/review
- Insurance
- Ground rent receipts
- Forfeiture provisions
- Unexpired term
- Notices
  - – Identify all notices that have to be served
  - – Upon whom they should be served
  - – The fee payable (check lease to see if specific sum payable)
  - – Make sure receipted copies of the relevant notices are obtained
- Obtain clear ground rent receipt

CHECKLIST **Conveyancing**

- Establish the identity of the client
- Obtain the authority to act from all the clients
- Have all the clients been met
- Rule 15 letter
- Retainer letter
- Conflict check
- Money laundering check
- What is the client buying
- Why is the client buying
- How is the client to fund the purchase
- Establish the intended use of the property
- Evidence to suggest any unusual aspects of the transaction, which may constitute a fraud
- Check client's instructions
- Explain terminology to client where appropriate, i.e. local authority search
- Submit all appropriate searches
- Read the results of the searches
- Advise client of any adverse entries
- Does the location of the property require any unusual searches to be undertaken (e.g. clay mining)

- Check validity of NHBC documentation where appropriate
- Check contract documentation
- Get plan approved by client
- Check estate agent particulars to identify potential discrepancies
- Check title documentation and report to client on fences/access/sewers and drainage and all other material matters relating to use and enjoyment of property
- Check planning of the property
- Has the property been altered or extended
- Were consents obtained
- Was work carried out in accordance with consents
- Is the property listed
- Check restrictive covenants affecting property – tell client
- Check through contract with client
- Check mortgage offer with clients
- How is property to be held – joint tenants or tenants in common
- Check draft completion statement figures with client
- Consider any tax implications that may affect the transaction (Capital Gains Tax)
- Confirm dates with client recompletion/exchange
- Comply with Rule 6 requirements in their entirety
- Exchange and report back to client asap
- Draft all documents with care
- Carry out all appropriate searches
- Ensure all appropriate undertakings are given/received
- Check all appropriate documents are signed prior to completion
- Are all completion statements correct
- Have all monies from client been received and cleared
- Submit application for registration within the appropriate timescales.
- Register any charges at Companies House within the appropriate timescale

---

CHECKLIST   **Landlord and tenant pitfalls**

- Using out-of-date or obsolete precedents
- Not communicating suggested amendments to the client and seeking instructions
- Not recording advice given and instructions received
- Not proofing the final draft and checking with client
- Not comparing final document with instructions received
- Failing to obtain appropriate consents to grants and alterations
- Inadequate or incorrect plans used
- Failing to advise on alienation clauses
- Inadequate advice on rent review clauses
- Not identifying and advising on tenant's obligations in the lease (repair, redecoration, etc.)

- Not meeting the time limits for service of notices pursuant to the Landlord and Tenant Act 1954
- Failing to deal effectively with options in a lease including registration, giving notice to exercise, and identifying and advising on preconditions

NB Many of the leasehold checks identified above apply as much to commercial issues as they do to residential

CHECKLIST **Litigation pitfalls**

- Limitation periods – this covers an enormous area. Limitation periods must be identified including unusual limitation periods both in the jurisdictions of England and Wales as well as abroad. Never make assumptions
- Failing to follow established protocols
- Costs – undertake a cost–benefit analysis, proportionality, prospects of recovery
- Failing to advise client of timetable, and ensuring that it is kept to
- Incorrect identification of parties to an action
- Failing to obtain adequate expert advice
- Not identifying and advising on all relevant issues
- Not managing client's expectations as to damages
- Failing to establish the location of defendant for service in sufficient time
- Failing to check accuracy of documents and pleadings with client prior to issue
- Failing to issue and serve within limitation periods
- Delaying on a file – failure to maintain momentum and ensure compliance with any timetable
- Failing to check client/witness availability for trial
- Agreeing variations to an agreed timetable and then overlooking the new date
- Failure to confirm instructions received or advice given in writing
- Failing to advise client of adverse costs orders
- Failing to enforce judgments within acceptable timescales

CHECKLIST   **Trust and probate pitfalls**

- Delay in drafting a will
- Will failing to reflect the client's instructions
- Not checking the title to property left in a will
- Failing to advise on tax issues
- Final will not proof-read
- Content of will not explained to client
- Incorrect attestation of will (i.e. beneficiary or spouse of beneficiary signing as witness)
- Loss of will while in the custody of the lawyer
- Delay generally and especially with regard to submission of tax returns (penalties) payment of legacies (interest) acting on instructions to sell (fall in stock market values or property)
- Overlooking payment of debts
- Failure to identify beneficiaries
- Incorrect payments to beneficiaries
- Not insuring empty dwelling house in estate, ensuring it is secured and cleared, and water system drained down if empty for prolonged period

---

CHECKLIST   **Commercial pitfalls**

- Failure to identify client company correctly and potential conflicts
- Not sending Rule 15 and retainer letters to clients
- Not confirming advice given or instructions received in writing
- Failing to identify and advise on tax issues
- Failing to check whether it is a share sale or an asset sale
- Ineffective communication with other experts (financiers, accountants or external consultants)
- Failing to establish which professional is doing what for the client
- Not advising on employment issues correctly or at all
- Failing to lodge charges at Companies House within the statutory period
- Failing to check documentation with the client
- Failing to check and proof-read final draft/engrossment

CHECKLIST   **Matrimonial pitfalls**

- Failing to obtain and act upon instructions from the client
- Not obtaining full disclosure of other spouse's assets
- Acting on out-of-date valuations
- Failing to advise on preservation of assets and severing joint tenancies where appropriate
- Non-compliance with Rule 15 and failing to advise client adequately or at all about costs
- Failing to advise on the remarriage trap
- Delay in a matter may lead to changed circumstances (inheritance/bonus received)
- Not checking draft consent order with client
- Failing to advise on pension or endowment policies. Failing to deal with assignments of such policies after order is made
- Failing to ensure all agreed terms are included in the final order
- Failing to ensure final order is made
- Not applying for a decree nisi to be made absolute
- Failing to advise of impact of remarriage/divorce on a will

Notes

1. This case was referred to by Tony Girling at a CLT conference on professional compliance issues in summer 2004.

9

Client relationships

- The initial interview
- The contents of advice
- Identify contact for client
- Communication with the client
- Dealing with complaints
- Dealing with claims
- Recording, analysis and remedial action

Managing the relationship with the client is fundamental to ensuring that the client receives a satisfactory level of service from the practice. The most common result from not so doing is a client who is unhappy with the practice and who is likely to tell other people of their poor experience. Complaints and claims could also easily, and quite needlessly, arise.

Many practices treat complaints and claims as separate issues, usually because responsibility for them might be split. In terms of operational risk management it is advisable to keep the distinction to a minimum. The Solicitors Indemnity Fund self-assessment risk audit states that it is the 'underlying cause' that should be concentrated on and not the distinction placed on it by the client or adviser. As that publication suggests – 'whether that occurrence is a complaint or a claim, frequently, is a matter of luck'.

EXAMPLE **Delay in carrying out instructions**

A solicitor receives instructions to draft a will on behalf of a client, and says it will be ready in a week. The solicitor delays and the draft is not prepared. The client rings up to ask where the draft is as the week has long since passed. The solicitor apologises and promises to get it out within 24 hours. In fact it is sent out three days later and contains a number of errors. The unhappy client returns the draft and eventually, after several more delays, the will is executed some two months after the original instructions were given. The client complains on receipt of the bill.

> The firm has received a complaint, but it might just as easily have been a claim if the client had died between the incorrect draft being returned and the will being engrossed in readiness for execution.

This example would suggest that not too much significance should be placed on the distinction between complaints and claims in firms where different processes exist. One device that often works well in such firms is to have a common reporting mechanism, with a partner responsible then deciding which procedure – complaint or claim – should be pursued. Lexcel provides at section 6.7a that there will need to be 'one overall risk manager' so that an overview can be taken of the firm's exposure to claims and complaints. This person should have 'sufficient seniority, to be able to identify and deal with all risk issues which may arise' and would usually be associated with the review of risk that has to be compiled at least annually under section 6.7f. The thrust of these provisions is that when things go wrong there ought to be clear responsibility for putting things right.

The potential for stress and misunderstanding is never too far away from most legal work. Clients tend to consult solicitors at times of crises – the death of a relative, a dispute or the breakdown of personal relationships. Moving house, likewise, can be a time of great stress and anxiety. Such situations do not bode well for a happy relationship and the firm that claims to have had no complaints for more than a year is probably suppressing the evidence. Key to any successful relationship is good, clear effective communication between solicitor and client. Solicitors often talk about 'unreasonable clients' expecting matters to be dealt with in 'unrealistic timescales' or having 'unreasonable expectations'. Most clients, however, will see themselves as making demands that are perfectly reasonable. The onus is on the solicitor to explain the process and disillusion them at the outset as to any unrealistic expectations that they may have.

The initial interview

Obtaining instructions can require considerable skill, especially if the client is not familiar with legal processes. It can be very difficult to elicit the necessary information from the client to enable the solicitor to advise correctly. The solicitor's task is to obtain all the relevant information from the client and then to advise the client so that they can make an informed decision as to what action they will take. In particularly complex matters the added risk is that some of the relevant information will not be asked for, and could be overlooked. Checklists can help and are increasingly used to assist in the interview process. It is important to remember, however, that such checklists are an *aide-mémoire* and not a substitute for the solicitor's skill and expertise.

When it comes to dispensing advice it is all too easy for solicitors to slip into legal phraseology and so baffle their client. A generation of lawyers have now been trained to avoid Latin terminology but it is often the more everyday legal language that can cause confusion. How does it sound to most clients to hear that documents must be 'lodged' at court, that clauses in a document can be 'boilerplated' or that the barrister that they are paying for needs 'daily refreshers'? Advice to 'execute a codicil' needs to be accompanied by an explanation of what a codicil is and the advantages of following such a course of action. Likewise, solicitors should not assume that clients will automatically understand how a conveyancing transaction proceeds, and so what is therefore meant by 'exchange of contracts', 'completion' and other such standard conveyancing phrases. A simple explanation at an early stage may avoid considerable problems later and many firms have now adopted very much more helpful client literature, which is generally appreciated by clients.

EXAMPLE   **Failure to explain 'local search'**

In one case a firm acted on behalf of a client in the purchase of a house. All appeared to go well and the matter completed. Some several months later the client wrote in complaining that he had just found out that there was a proposal to build a bypass, which his property would overlook. There was also the question of the increased noise. The solicitor checked the file and the search revealed no entries. It transpired that the bypass was sufficiently far away not to warrant an entry in the search. The client was told and it was explained that while the search was called a 'local search' in fact it only searched the property itself and in the immediate vicinity in respect of certain other matters. The client asked why he had not been told that at the outset, as he had assumed that local search meant what it said, i.e. a search of the local area.

The client must be asked if there are any particular timescales to which the client wishes to work, and once identified, the client should be told if these are not realistic, and, most important, why. Timescales are also an issue dealt with by professional rules – the Solicitors' Costs Information and Client Code requiring 'a clear explanation of the issues raised in a matter . . . (including the likely timescale)' (para.7(a)(i)).

These are provisions that are imported into Lexcel, since compliance with the Code is required by section 7.1b of the standard, but the point on timescale also appears as one of the issues to be confirmed to the client in the list of points at section 8.4 (see Chapter 6, p.77). The section goes on to state that these issues must be confirmed to the client 'ordinarily in writing', but subject to the exceptions permitted under the Code.

The client should be advised of any specific dates such as court hearings, limitation or notice periods that will have to be observed or met in the course of the retainer. Key dates are dealt with under Lexcel at section 8.7b which provides that they must be 'recorded on the file and in a back-up system'. Agreeing a timetable with the client for progressing the matter is also recommended.

The contents of advice

Client expectations need to be managed from the outset as failure to do so will often result in a disappointed client at a later date. Better by far to deal with the bad news in advance rather than when the client has failed to receive the amount of damages that they had anticipated or their costs are out of line with expectations. The skill is to introduce the worst likely outcome to the client without sounding defeatist or downbeat. Clients who are disappointed with the outcome of their matter can easily develop into clients who complain or make a claim for damages. It may well be that there is no merit to the complaint or claim that is forthcoming but time will have to be taken to deal with it nonetheless.

As soon as the solicitor is in possession of all the facts, clear advice should be given as to the merits of the case. The client will inevitably want to know as soon as possible what the likely outcome will be, but it will often be better not to be hurried into a premature assessment that later has to be downgraded. The initial interview might be too early to make an assessment of the client's prospects of success, in which case the client should be told what research is necessary and when this might be completed. If there will be a delay the client needs to be warned and also provided with an indication of the likely costs that will be incurred in getting to that position.

Identify contact for client

Even where teams share responsibility for clients it tends to be standard practice to designate one person as the point of contact for that client. The Solicitors' Costs Information and Client Care Code (at para.7(a)(ii)) requires that the client should be:

> given the name and status of the person dealing with the matter and the name of the principal, or director (in the case of a recognised body which is a company), or member (in the case of a recognised body which is a limited liability partnership) responsible for its overall supervision; . . .

There are similar requirements to these provisions at Rule 2.02 in the new draft rules. The case that should still be of concern on confirming the name and status of the adviser is *Pearless de Rougemont & Co v. Pilbrow (No. 2)* [1999] 3 All ER 355. The client asked for a solicitor to advise him on his divorce. The evidence suggested that there was a breakdown of communication between the reception services and the family law department, resulting in the client being advised by an experienced, but unadmitted, adviser. Discovering this fact late on in the matter, the client refused to pay for his legal advice and was successfully sued by the firm. The Court of Appeal overturned this decision, mostly on grounds that advice from a non-solicitor was a 'different thing in kind' from advice from a solicitor, which is what the client had expressly requested. This being so there was no *quantum meruit* claim and there was no obligation on the part of the client to pay for the firm's services even though the manner in which the case had been conducted could not be questioned. The firm therefore found itself in the doubly disadvantaged position of receiving no fees for the matter and having to meet the costs of a successful appeal against it to the Court of Appeal.

Views on this case differ, but critics would say that this decision overlooks the obligation of the partners in a practice to supervise all work done within the firm. Had there been deficiencies in the advice provided, the partners would have been liable. Since all correspondence from the firm is in the name of the partners it is difficult to see how the identity of the adviser could fairly be said to be so different from advice from a solicitor colleague in the same department. Whatever the arguments about this decision, the importance of confirming details as to the person handling the matter and the principal or partner responsible for it should not be overlooked. On this latter point, by the way, the Practice Standards Unit commonly finds that the person named for overall supervision is an employee – perhaps a legal executive who heads up the conveyancing department. The professional rules do make it clear that the overall supervisor has to have the status of principal, partner or equivalent in the firm.

Changes of adviser are bound to occur from time to time, but are a regular and guaranteed source of annoyance to clients – more so where the fee earner dealing with the matter is replaced without notice by someone else within the practice. Although this point is not specifically dealt with by the professional conduct rules, Lexcel has a provision at section 8.7e that clients must be 'informed in writing if the person with conduct of their matter changes, or there is a change of person to whom any problem with service should be addressed'. Ideally the client should be consulted about changes of personnel and their views on the issue should be sought. In similar vein, delegation that the client was not expecting can cause problems. The most common examples involve clients who are initially dealt with by a partner, only to discover at a later stage that their work has now been delegated to a more junior fee earner without adequate explanation.

To prevent these situations arising the practice should appoint a client partner who is the focal point for the client at the practice. This is the person whom the client may contact if he or she is unhappy with any aspect of the relationship with the practice. It does not have to be the same person named in the Rule 15 letter to contact in the event that the client is dissatisfied with the service received. It is for this partner to manage the relationship with the client in a proactive manner. Simply to pick up the phone and ask the client how everything is going can have a major positive impact on the client and conveys a message to the client that the practice cares.

The case plan – or matter planner – identifies what needs to be done and how it will be achieved, also by when and by whom (Lexcel, section 8.5). Although usually little more than the letter confirming instructions to the client, it may need to be more elaborate in more major matters and there are provisions requiring a 'separate case plan' in certain high cost and multi-claimant legal aid cases (SQM 2002, section F2.1). Ideally a case plan should set out the client's instructions to reduce the risk of overlooking any instructions on a particular issue, and identify and remove any confusion between adviser and client on the scope of the retainer. The main steps to achieve the desired outcome should also appear, including critical dates and time limits. Highlighting such information on the file reduces the risk of overlooking a key step or date at a later stage. The planned timescale is also important, as are any points on the personnel involved.

Communication with the client

It was stated earlier in this chapter that communication is the foundation upon which the client relationship is based. Many of the complaints made against solicitors stem from poor communication and it is therefore worth adopting clear procedures that deal with it. The key principles are as follows.

Keep the client advised as to what is happening on a regular basis

If nothing has happened on the file then advise the client that this is the case, together with an explanation as to why nothing has happened. The intervals between communication will be governed by the type of work involved and it will be for the relevant departmental heads to decide what is appropriate. If a timescale has been set out in the engagement letter, it is important that it is adhered to.

Response times

Many firms choose to include set response times in their client literature – the most common examples are to return phone calls within 24 hours and reply to correspondence within two days. There is no obligation to do this but the Lexcel guidance states that where a firm has set such a response time, this is the standard to which they will be assessed in determining if progress has been satisfactorily maintained under section 8.7c, which requires that a 'timely response is made to telephone calls and correspondence'.

Advice given to the client should be confirmed in writing

This may be done by way of a letter, an e-mail or an attendance note copied to the client. There should be a procedure in the practice relating to letters of advice. They should be checked and signed off by a partner, or by an authorised signatory who has had the appropriate authority delegated to them after proper enquiry by the partners. Advice in writing is difficult to challenge at a later date, and reduces the likelihood of success of the client alleging poor, inadequate or wrong advice, which may arise some years later. Sadly, the watchword of advisers should be always to 'cover your back'.

Plain English

There is no substitute for clear language. When writing to the client, care should be taken to ensure that the letter is to the point and concise, and written in easy-to-follow English. The test is not that the solicitor understands the letter, but that the client does. It should also be stressed that clear layout can considerably assist comprehension, especially where the advice needs to be lengthy or is complex.

Regular updates as to costs

This is a matter dealt with by professional rules and was examined in Chapter 8 but its importance cannot be overstated. Failures of costs information are the cause of innumerable complaints, and a common failing in compliance terms in relation to the Solicitors' Costs Information and Client Care Code. The amount of a bill should never take the client by surprise.

Deeds and documents

The content of a document should always be explained to the client before the client signs. In order to be effective, certain documents have to be drawn in a particular way that does not make them client friendly – wills being the most obvious example. This does not however obviate the need to explain the document. Time should be taken to talk the client through the trust clauses in a will, or the rent review clauses in a lease and explain what they mean and the implications of the particular clause. This should be done in private and not in the reception area, where other clients may be sitting. The client is entitled to understand the process that they find themselves involved in and will then be more likely to identify any potential errors or omissions in the document.

Attendance notes are essential

When instructions are received, or advice given, then the advice and instructions should be confirmed either in a letter (see above) or in an attendance note. Practitioners in certain disciplines are more accomplished at making attendance notes than others. Litigation solicitors are generally more assiduous in this regard, while corporate advisers tend to be more cavalier. The excuse commonly put forward by the latter is that there is simply not time to make such notes in the course of a busy completion meeting. It is important that time is made. If the client alleges that he instructed his solicitor to do something or that he was given a particular piece of advice that has subsequently caused him loss, evidence on the file will be needed to refute the allegation. The judiciary have a tendency, in the absence of such evidence, to prefer the client's testimony to the solicitor's. This is not necessarily because the judge disbelieves the solicitor – more likely is the view that solicitors are often involved in numerous transactions at the same time and the client only in one, and therefore the client's recollection of events is probably more reliable.

Standard letters

Standard drafts are an effective communication aid in that they can address advice commonly dispensed to clients on issues such as the relative merits and demerits of holding property as joint tenants or tenants in common, the duties of executors and trustees, and the effect of remarriage or divorce on wills. Where these are printed leaflets the file should clearly record when they were sent to the client and which version was used.

Dealing with complaints

Inevitably there will be occasions when the relationship between solicitor and client breaks down, but this need not mean that the relationship has come to an end. An effective response to a problem will often result in its early resolution and a satisfied client. There is even evidence to suggest that a difficulty that is well dealt with increases client satisfaction – i.e. the client is more pleased with the service than if a problem had never arisen in the first place. An ineffective response may mean the problem will continue and grow worse and even become irreparable. This is when claims or complaints tend to arise.

Complaints procedure

All firms in private practice are required to have a written complaints procedure in place. The requirements are found in the Solicitors' Costs Information and Client Care Code at paragraph 7, which provides that the client is told 'whom to approach about any problem with the service provided', that there must be a 'written complaints procedure' and that 'the client is given a copy of the complaints procedure on request'. There is an obligation to ensure that complaints are handled in accordance with the written complaints procedure. The new draft professional rules make similar requirements but add for the first time the requirement that the complainant should be told how their communication will be dealt with and to what timescale (see Rule 2.04).

There remains a common misconception that the full complaints procedure has to be set out in the Rule 15 letter, but this has never been the case under Law Society rules. Earlier versions of legal aid Franchising standards did require this and even though the SQM is more ambivalent on the point, some assessors do still insist on the full procedure being set out at the outset. Section G1.1 of that standard talks about the need for 'work practices' to show that 'clients have information about what to do if they have a problem with the services provided'. Any suggestion that this could be limited to ensuring that the client knows the appropriate person to contact if a problem does arise is put into doubt by the explanation in the SQM that this means that firms 'must provide details of how and to whom to complain'. Unfortunately the guidance document that accompanies the SQM does not really throw further light on the subject.

Whatever the approach of legal aid assessors on this point, the Practice Standards Unit of the Law Society advises against setting out the full complaints procedure at the outset. The wording in the Solicitors' Costs Information and Client Care Code makes it clear that as long as the adviser deals with the issue of 'whom to contact about any problem with the service provided' (para.7(a)(iii)) they will have met their responsibilities. The Law Society also recommends that the client care letter does not refer to 'a complaint' but is more subtle. An acceptable wording would therefore be:

> ABC & Co endeavour to provide a quality service to our clients. In the event that you are disappointed with our service or feel that there are issues that

you would like to discuss please raise this with your fee earner/adviser or alternatively please contact A – the departmental head/managing partner/ other to discuss the matter further.

The complaints procedure will need to make provisions for how the matter will be dealt with by the practice and to whom the complaint will be referred internally if the client is still not satisfied. Although this person is normally styled the 'complaints partner', this term should be avoided with clients for much the same reasons as the word 'complaint' should be avoided in the initial letter to the client. Every practice must, however, have a nominated complaints partner who will be responsible for overseeing the practice's complaints procedure and who will usually be the ultimate arbiter within the practice's internal procedure. It should be noted that a growing number of firms have an appeals level above this person and this is a service that a number of local law societies have developed in recent years with some considerable success. While the complaints partner is able to delegate responsibility for dealing with a complaint to another individual within the practice, he or she cannot delegate accountability. If a complaint is delegated to another partner and is not dealt with properly then it is the complaints partner who will be accountable to the Consumer Complaints Service and perhaps ultimately to the Solicitors Disciplinary Tribunal.

It is important that the person who is appointed complaints partner has the requisite skills and authority to discharge the function effectively. Solicitors tend to deal with matters in a confrontational manner. One report termed the approach adopted by many firms as 'quasi-judicial'.[1] When a complaint is received it is as if the onus is on the client to show, on the balance of probabilities, that they have been let down in some way by the firm. In many firms the adviser is consulted in person but not the client. The file is examined and the client then receives a letter stating that a thorough review has shown that there is 'no cause for concern'. The client feels patronised and alienated. They may abandon the process there – highly dissatisfied with the firm and now bad-mouthing it at every opportunity, or they may take the matter further. Better by far, argued that report, to take a commercial view and accept that the client – right or wrong – is dissatisfied. Acknowledging this to be a fact and exploring what can reasonably be done to put things right is a better and more realistic strategy for damage limitation.

The objective with any complaint must be to deal with it as quickly and effectively as possible. People tend to express dissatisfaction when they perceive that they are not receiving the level of service that they feel they are entitled to. If a client feels this way it indicates a failing on the part of the solicitor. For example, if a telephone call is not returned the same day, that fact might seem of no consequence to the solicitor, but of considerable importance to the client. The client might have been extremely anxious to speak with the solicitor and waited in all day for the return call. It is crucial in any service industry that the service supplier sees matters from the customer's point of view: if the customer is not happy there is usually a reason for it.

Lexcel

In relation to complaints handling Lexcel mostly reaffirms the requirements of the Solicitors' Costs Information and Client Care Code:

> Practices will operate a written complaints handling procedure that:
>
> a: Is made readily available and accessible to clients when it is apparent that they may wish to have recourse to it.
> b: Defines what the practice regards as a complaint and sets out how to identify and respond to complaints.
> c: Records and reports centrally all complaints received from clients.
> d: Identifies the cause of any problem of which the client has complained, offering any appropriate redress, and correcting any unsatisfactory procedures.
>
> Lexcel, section 7.3

The requirement that a practice needs to define what it understands to be a complaint recognises that a wide or narrow view can be taken on the point. It is of some significance when its effect on section 7.3c is taken into account. The firm that defines a complaint in wide terms such as 'any expression of client dissatisfaction, however expressed'[2] will find itself reporting problems that have been dealt with at the time by the adviser and to the client's apparent satisfaction. An alternative (narrow) definition could be 'any expression of client dissatisfaction which the adviser is unable immediately to resolve'. This offers a common-sense filter for the everyday anxieties that will be expressed during the legal process and can therefore mean that the firm is more focused on the genuine problems that do arise.

It should also be noted that a review of complaints is needed under section 7.3 and is required to form part of an overall review of risk exposure under section 6.7f of the standard.

Adequate training should be provided for those individuals in the practice who are responsible for dealing with complaints. It should hardly be surprising to conclude that too many solicitors approach complaints on a semi-litigious basis since this is what they do in their professional lives but it is important that complaints about service delivery are not dealt with in this manner. Recognising this, many firms have employed non-solicitors to deal with complaints under the supervision of the complaints partner.

Dealing with claims

One of the major changes with the advent of the open market for indemnity insurance was the change in the requirements for notifying a claim to insurers. Broadly, under the old rules, a solicitor was obliged to notify the Solicitors Indemnity Fund only in the event of a claim. Under the 'minimum terms and conditions' that approved insurers are obliged to observe the obligation is more onerous. The requirement is that any circumstance that may *give rise to* a claim must be notified to insurers.

It is important that all relevant staff in a practice are fully aware of their obligations in this regard. When a circumstance arises it should be notified immediately to the relevant partner and not 'stored up' for a mass notification immediately prior to renewal. Some practices send a memo around once a year asking fee earners to identify any circumstances. This is not recommended since it is likely to encourage late notification. This arises when a set of circumstances arises in one year of indemnity and is notified in a subsequent year. If this were to happen, although the insurer would be under a responsibility to deal with the claim and pay any damages, the insurer may have the right to recover from the partners of the practice sums equivalent to any payments made. This is the case even if the practice remains with the same insurer over the period.

Recording, analysis and remedial action

It is important for practices to learn from past mistakes and complaints, and see how they can improve on their service delivery to the client. Irrespective of whether the mistake gives rise to a complaint or a claim, what matters is to record and analyse the event. The Lexcel standard requires this by means of an annual risk review (section 6.7f).

The first step is to analyse what went wrong. This will mean identifying the underlying cause of the complaint or the claim. The underlying causes of claim have already been identified in Chapter 3. The underlying causes of complaints as identified by Mike Frith – for many years Senior Caseworker and Compliance Officer at the then Office for Supervision of Solicitors – as:

- failing to manage expectations;
- poor use of language, for example inappropriate use of jargon;
- defective costs information;
- delay/failure to keep the client informed;
- failure to reply to client communication;
- incorrect advice, in which case claims might also arise.

There will doubtless be some other causes of complaints, but these are the principal offenders. The fee earner responsible for the problem should be involved in the analysis, as it will be necessary to identify not only what went wrong, but why. It may be necessary to consider whether the fee earner's past work needs to be audited to ascertain if there are any other problems. Further steps should be taken once the cause has been established and analysed to ensure that there is no repetition or at least that the risk of such a repetition has been reduced to an acceptable level. The remedial action to be taken should be implemented within a specified timescale and supervised by a nominated individual, such as the risk manager, to ensure that the action is completed.

A central record needs to be kept of these events, both complaints and claims. The record should contain the following information:

- the complainant/claimant;
- the department, section team, etc., concerned;
- the date of the incident;
- what happened;
- why it happened;
- whether the practice was wholly or partly to blame;
- whether a similar action by the same person could have given rise to similar problems in the past;
- the amount claimed when known, with time costs evaluated separately (see below);
- the loss to be borne by the practice;
- the member of staff alleged to be responsible for causing the risk event.[3]

The costs of dealing with a complaint or a claim can be substantial in terms of both write-offs of bills and management time, and some firms therefore set these costs off against departmental budgets. There is often resistance to this, since the view is taken that it might discourage fee earners from notifying circumstances. This is unlikely as a fee earner is just as likely to withhold notifying a circumstance for a number of other reasons, not least of all their own reputation. If the culture of the practice is supportive, however, there should not be any problem. In any event, a practice must know how much claims and complaints are costing in financial terms, as it will impact on the firm's profit. Simply placing a reserve in the accounts to meet the excess liability is unlikely to tell the whole story.

> EXAMPLE   **Breakdown of cost of claim**
>
> One practice undertook a detailed costing exercise of a claim relating to a tripping accident. The amount of the claim was £35,000, but the cost to the practice was £50,000. The practice returned all of the fees paid by the client, and the balance of the additional costs consisted of the partner's time in dealing with the matter and that of the fee earner responsible, as well as the additional loading that the claim attracted to the following year's premium.

The final step in the remedial process is to decide what further action may need to be taken in respect of the individual responsible for the claim. The analysis might show that it was not a failure on the part of the individual but a failure on the part of the practice's processes and procedures, in which case no further action will be required in respect of the individual. Alternatively, a training issue may be identified, which needs to be addressed with the individual.

An increasing number of firms make a review of complaints and claims received an issue in the practice's appraisal process. Where this is the case it is important to ensure that the appraisal system does not take on a disciplinary feel to it. One way to safeguard against this risk is to review all feedback received and not just the more negative data from complaints and claims. In some cases there may be a competence issue or disciplinary action required. This is the last resort, however, and could clearly discourage openness. It will be preferable to subject the adviser to a greater degree of supervision. Ultimately, of course, if an individual has failed to follow the procedures, ignored the risk, and acted in a reckless manner that has cost the practice a very considerable amount of money, the practice needs to consider whether it is in the best interests of the practice and its clients to continue to employ that person.

Notes

1   C. Christensen, S. Worthington and J. Day, 'An investigation into in-house complaint handling by solicitors', 1998.
2   This remains the wording suggested by the SQM although it is not mandatory – see guidance document to SQM at p.105.
3   Source: SIF self-assessment questionnaire 2000.

10

File closure

KEY POINTS

- Termination of the retainer
- File closure procedures
- File storage and destruction
- Storage of clients' deeds and documents

In many respects achieving a clear end to the retainer is just as important as stamping clear control over it at the outset. The client's last impression of the service that they receive is the one that is most likely to influence their future choice of advisers and most firms will depend heavily on repeat business from existing clients. Sadly, the solicitor–client relationship frequently descends into administrative chaos at the end of the matter: the more interesting substantive work has been finished and all that is left to do is to tie up the loose ends and close the file. Delays in processing the work at this stage can be just as frustrating for the client as earlier in the work, however, and can lead to an array of complaints and claims. It must be remembered that the duty of care of the solicitor continues until such time as the retainer is terminated, and that will only happen when all outstanding issues have been dealt with properly.

More often than not, file closure is regarded as being an essentially administrative task and is therefore entrusted to a junior fee earner or a secretary. If such people are left to get on with things with little or no supervision, errors can easily arise. It may well make sense to delegate files at this stage but this should not be the end of the fee earner's involvement with them. Delegation of activities is not the same thing as abdication of responsibility and the adoption of a clear file closing procedure can ensure that the task is handled both competently and efficiently.

Termination of the retainer

Ordinarily, work will be completed before the retainer can be discharged. However, there are limited circumstances in which the retainer can be terminated by the solicitor.

The Guide sets out examples of when a retainer may be terminated, including:

- where continuing to act would be in breach of the rules or principles of conduct;
- where the solicitor is unable to obtain any clear instructions from the client;
- where there is a serious breakdown in confidence between the solicitor and the client;
- by operation of law (i.e. by reason of the solicitor's/client's bankruptcy).

Even when the solicitor does have good grounds for termination, he or she may only do so on giving reasonable notice. It would not therefore be permissible to compromise the client, for example by terminating on the day of the hearing because of non-payment of costs. Since the solicitor will be obliged in most cases to continue to represent the client unless there are clear grounds for doing otherwise, the importance of client selection is readily apparent. By contrast, the client is at liberty to terminate the retainer at any time.

Care also needs to be taken when proposing to terminate a retainer for non-payment of costs on account. This is an area that frequently causes problems. There is an assumption that if a payment on account is requested and not received then the solicitor is at liberty to terminate the retainer. Reference needs to be made to Principle 14.01 of the Guide on this point. In non-contentious matters the solicitor must make any requirement for a payment on account of costs, as distinct from disbursements, a condition of accepting instructions. In the absence of such a condition, the solicitor is not entitled to terminate the retainer if the client refuses to make a payment. This may have serious implications for the solicitor from a financial point of view, quite apart from the strained relationships with the client that such a situation is likely to engender. A clear provision in the terms and conditions entitling the solicitor to terminate the relationship is clearly advisable. The situation is different in contentious matters. Where a solicitor makes a request for a *reasonable* sum on account of costs, and the client refuses or fails within a reasonable time to make that payment, the solicitor is entitled to terminate the retainer upon giving reasonable notice.

Often where a retainer is terminated on one of the above grounds, costs will remain outstanding, and solicitors will exercise a lien over the client's papers until such time as the costs are paid. Again, care needs to be taken. The Guide seems supportive on this point:

It is not unprofessional for a solicitor to retain papers and property belonging to the client, pending payment of professional costs owed by that client, where the retention is a proper exercise of a solicitor's lien.

The Guide, Principle 12.14

The lien will be challengeable, however, unless the solicitor either delivers a bill or gives the client sufficient particulars to enable them to calculate the amount owing. A pragmatic view should be taken where a dispute develops. If a client makes allegations as to the standard of service that he or she has received, or indicates that they may wish to make a claim, exercising a lien is only going to complicate the situation. The client could make an application to the court for an order that the papers are delivered up so as to enable the client to pursue the matter, and on most occasions the court is likely to order in their favour. Frequently in such situations there will be an order that the papers are delivered to the client against an undertaking from the client's new solicitors as to outstanding costs. The Guide suggests that in such situations the former solicitor should keep a complete copy of the file to enable any subsequent complaint or claim to be dealt with effectively, and for record keeping purposes.

Disputes notwithstanding, in most cases the retainer will come to an end when the bill is paid and the file closed. In order to ensure that this process is achieved with the minimum exposure to the risk of an error, it is suggested that there is a clearly defined process to be followed.

File closure procedures

It is the practical steps involved in terminating the file that Lexcel tends to concentrate on. The issue is covered at section 8.11. This provides a useful checklist of the main issues to be dealt with to bring any matter to a close.

Practices will have documented procedures to ensure that, at the end of the matter, the practice:

a: Reports to the client on the outcome and explains any further action that the client is required to take in the matter and what (if anything) the practice will do.

b: Accounts to the client for any outstanding money.

c: Returns to the client any original documents or other property belonging to the client if required (save for items, which are by agreement to be stored by the practice).

d: If appropriate, advises the client about arrangements for storage and retrieval of papers and other items retained (in so far as this has not already been dealt with, for example in terms of business) and any charges to be made in this regard.

e: Advises the client whether they should review the matter in future and, if so, when and why.

f: Archives or destroys files in an appropriate manner.

Domestic conveyancing

The area of domestic conveyancing probably best illustrates the importance of clear file closure procedures. The momentum to progress matters on a file after completion falters, as the client is in his or her new home and the estate agent has been paid, so there is no one chasing the solicitor to submit the application for registration, or serve the appropriate notices pursuant to the terms of the lease, or submit the Stamp Duty Land Tax (SDLT) form.

> EXAMPLE   **Failure to register within priority period of search**
>
> A completed the purchase on behalf of his client within extremely short timescales. The client was extremely pleased with A and said he would be 'recommending him to all his friends'. A turned his attention to other matters and eventually got round to submitting the application for registration. The lenders were beginning to chase the firm for progress updates and wanting to know why they had not received confirmation of the completion of the registration.
>
> The application was eventually sent in some considerable while after the priority period afforded by the HMLR search. It transpired that the seller had owed considerable sums of money. Entries in favour of creditors had been made on the register after completion and before A had submitted his application for registration. Enquiries of the seller's solicitors revealed that they had no contact address for the client and were without instructions. The creditors refused to remove their entries.
>
> A said that he had submitted registrations out of time on numerous occasions before and never had a problem. Had A maintained the momentum on the file after completion and submitted the application within the priority period then the claim would never had arisen.

The above example suggests that it might be sensible to adapt the sort of general file closure checklist found in the *Lexcel Office Procedures Manual* (see the final review check on the File Summary Sheet at Appendix 8D) and develop more detailed checklists for particular work types. On this basis a residential conveyancing post-completion checklist might include the following:

- Obtain all documents from the seller's solicitors and check they are correct, have been signed, and that the necessary undertakings have been enclosed.
- Diarise ahead the expiration date of the HMLR search and a bring forward date to see if undertakings complied with.
- Attend to SDLT requirements.
- Attend to any undertakings given on buyer's behalf, i.e. repay loans for deposit to bank, parents or other lending source.
- Ensure Land Registry form DS1 received in respect of each mortgage.
- Submit application to HMLR within the priority period.
- Deal with any communications/requisitions received by HMLR expeditiously.
- Ensure all appropriate notices are served (pursuant to terms of lease and any guarantees affecting the property).
- Check completed HMLR application has been processed correctly (i.e. correct spelling of name, address and appropriate entries made such as tenants in common restriction).
- Comply with the lender's requirements re documentation.

This list should not be taken to be exhaustive, but it does demonstrate the sort of issues that need to be dealt with after completion and before the file may be safely stored away.

All work types

Other departments may well find their time is well used in drawing up lists similar to the domestic conveyancing one. It need not be too lengthy a task to undertake: a half-hour discussion at a departmental meeting should identify what needs to be included. Issues that should always be considered include the following:

- Check the original retainer letter and any subsequent amending letters to ensure that the client's instructions have been complied with.
- Ensure that all outstanding matters have been dealt with (i.e. such points as would be addressed by the work-specific checklist).
- Are there any further steps to be undertaken on behalf of the client (for example exercise of an option, rent review, or completion of future tax returns)?
- Have the client's expectations been met? Review how the practice has performed in the client's eyes.
- Carry out a risk review of the file.
- Check the client ledgers are clear.
- Has all time been billed or the necessary adjustments made?
- Check the file for file management purposes.
- Submit final report to the client.

- Decide on file destruction date.
- Archive the file.

Errors and omissions

The starting point in any closing review is to examine again what the solicitor originally agreed to do for the client and check whether it has been done. Reference to the retainer letter and any subsequent updates will assist the solicitor in checking that the agreed matters have all been attended to.

This check may reveal errors that have come to light after the transaction has been finalised. It may be too late to rectify an omission, as where a corporate transaction has completed and an asset has not been transferred to a particular subsidiary. However, the earlier a problem is identified the greater the prospects of putting things right.

In other cases the check may reveal omissions that can be rectified with the minimum of effort now but which, if not dealt with immediately or overlooked, could present insurmountable problems at a later date. In a complex private client matter, for example, instructions might include the preparation of a codicil. The codicil may have been overlooked while the solicitor was dealing with the client's tax and trust affairs. The omission is low risk if identified early on and rectified but problems could arise if the codicil was not prepared and the client died in the meantime. At that stage the matter would almost certainly be incapable of rectification. Any work type-based checklist will help to identify those common issues that tend to be overlooked when dealing with a matter. Checking the retainer letter will identify specific issues that the solicitor was instructed to deal with, whereas the work-specific checklist addresses those items that arise in any matter of that description and therefore might not necessarily be covered in the retainer letter.

Ongoing issues

It is important that there is clarity on the part of both the solicitor and the client with regard to ongoing obligations and who will deal with them. Numerous claims have been brought as a result of confusion as to responsibility for future action, especially in property work. The most common situations involve the grant of commercial leases where the solicitor acts on behalf of the tenant. If the lease contains an option to renew in favour of the tenant, which has to be exercised within a particular timescale that is missed, questions often arise as to whose responsibility it was to take the necessary action. In order to avoid any confusion it should be clearly established at completion of the lease whether the solicitor will be dealing with the option or if it will be the client's responsibility. By obtaining such clarification any future confusion on the part of the client and the solicitor should be avoided. If it is agreed that the solicitor will undertake work on the file at a later date it is crucial that this is entered on to a central key dates diary system and that details of what has to be done and when are recorded on the file in case that particular fee earner subsequently leaves the firm or is absent from the office at that stage for any reason.

Feedback

While perhaps not specifically a risk issue, obtaining client feedback is an integral part of the file closure procedure and is now a requirement (though not on all files) of Lexcel at section 7.4. It is impossible to ascertain accurately how successful the practice is at service delivery unless the client is asked. The practice may well feel that it is achieving commendably high standards of service delivery but the clients might not agree. Assessing client feedback can be 'qualitative', as where commercial clients are interviewed after a deal for their reaction to the service provide, or the simpler 'quantitative' client satisfaction surveys. For an example of a sample client satisfaction survey form see the *Lexcel Office Procedures Manual* at Appendix 7F.

Collecting information in this way is one thing but analysing it is often another. Asking questions of consumers of any business for their reactions raises the expectation that something will be done to put things right. It follows that someone should have the responsibility to monitor responses and ensure that there is a quick response on any marked statement of dissatisfaction. In all cases the feedback needs to be checked to identify areas for improvement and also to identify any underlying problems with a particular department, team or individual. This will enable steps to be taken to rectify matters before they lead to complaints and claims. It is equally important to celebrate positive feedback and the relevant staff should be informed and congratulated. Sharing praise and good news has an obvious and immediate effect on morale. Good working practices identified by the feedback should be highlighted to the other departments and adopted.

Risk analysis

As previously mentioned, a risk analysis of the matter needs to be conducted as part of the client acquisition process. It is equally important that risk is monitored throughout the life of the file and that a general review of risk is conducted at the file closure stage. Any complaints or claims need to be identified, as do any 'near misses' so that they may be analysed and any lessons learned. A closing review will also show whether the risk exposure assessed at the outset has increased at any stage in the retainer by reason of new instructions. If an increased level of risk has not been identified this may demonstrate a lack of adequate supervision or understanding of risk on the part of the fee earner.

Accounts

Although an apparently mundane issue, office and client ledger balances must be cleared at the end of the transaction. It may be true that balances should clear themselves if the statements have been carefully and correctly drafted but experience is often quite different. Having a number of small balances on various ledgers risks a breach of the professional rules and so could incur substantial costs for the practice and reputational damage. Costs will be incurred in dealing with the annual observation raised by the practice's auditors in the Solicitors' Accounts Rules reports highlighting the balances, the numerous unnecessary reports generated by the accounts department highlighting the balances and the amount of fee earner time spent trying to resolve the balances at a later date. Credit balances belong to the client and should be accounted for to the client as soon as possible. It is the client's money not the practice's. Following the file closure procedure will assist the fee earner in identifying these balances as soon as possible, enabling them to be dealt with expeditiously.

EXAMPLE   **Aged credit balances**

ABC & Co was a specialist property firm undertaking both residential and commercial transactions. Following their audit the firm's accountants indicated that the frequency of aged credit balances, and in some cases the size, were now of such a concern that the accountants were considering whether or not to qualify the firm's accounts. The firm then immediately embarked on an exercise to clear all the balances. Some went back five years. Initially the firm thought of writing the balances off. They were advised that this was not possible in most cases owing to the size of the balance. Many hours of fee earning time were lost as attempts were made to contact former clients, some of whom had died, or could not be traced, or in the case of corporate clients, simply no longer existed. Even in these cases the balances could not be written off and the Law Society procedure had to be followed whereby the balances were donated to the Solicitors Benevolent Association. It was accepted by ABC & Co that the time, resources and financial cost of this exercise were wholly disproportionate to any benefit that may have been gained. Thereafter client balances were closely monitored and fee earners were required to action and report back to accounts within three days of being notified of any small balances in the aged balance report.

From the firm's point of view it is important to make sure that all time recorded is accounted for and, where appropriate, billed. Again this needs to be done as soon as possible after completion of the retainer. The longer the period of time between the work being carried out and an invoice submitted, the less likely the client is to pay.

Many firms audit files at closure to ensure that they have been maintained in accordance with the practice's procedures. There is an obvious logic in checking files at this stage since the audit will then address all parts of the file management procedures. A failure to do so might mean that file closing processes are never checked. In legal aid audits – contract compliance audits most obviously – closed files are frequently checked. This suggests that the firm should be prepared to do the same. Checks can cover filing of correspondence, draft documents, marking of files, and whether there is an audit trail of financial transactions on the file. Furthermore, if case management plans or checklists are used by the practice, they should have been completed and acted upon. The file should also be checked to ensure that it has been thinned out in readiness for archiving. This is dealt with in more detail below.

Final report to client

The final report to the client provides the opportunity to address any outstanding items and to report to the client that the matter has been concluded and that the papers are being filed. The client feedback form might be included with the letter and it might also address the question of any future action to be undertaken and by whom, for example the exercise of an option. Any documents that belong to the client should be returned and the client advised as to what will happen with his or her file regarding future storage. This letter would provide a useful focal point for dealing with many of the matters set out in this section on file closure procedures.

File storage and destruction

Deciding on a destruction date is an integral part of the archiving process. The file destruction date needs to be selected by the fee earner, and where necessary signed off by the supervising partner. It should never be left to an archiving administrator to decide when a file should be destroyed.

It is important to remember that the papers belong to the client and that clients should be advised of the practice's destruction policy. It could be that the client will wish to retain his or her own papers, in which case they are entitled to do so and the papers should be sent to the client upon request. In such cases a full copy of the file should be retained by the practice.

A number of practices address file destruction with the client in their standard terms and conditions and have a pre-printed clause stating when the file will be destroyed. How long a file should be kept is a vexed question. There are a number of possible answers. A blanket destruction policy of 15 years at minimum to cover the longstop limitation period of latent claims might be the safest approach, but has cost implications in terms of file storage. Most firms conclude that the cost of maintaining most files for this sort of time is not merited given the likelihood of such claims arising. As an alternative, each file might have its own destruction date allocated to it depending on the subject matter for the file. This is the approach that is likely to be adopted by the more cost-conscious solicitor.

Where the solicitor has acted for the client in the sale of a property and no linked purchase, if there is a problem then it is likely to come to light at a very early date. In this situation the decision may be to destroy the file on the expiration of the primary limitation period, in which case it is advisable to keep the file for seven years as opposed to six. This will cater for the possibility that a claim form is issued on the cusp of limitation and then served after the expiration of the six-year limitation period. It is also important that the correct limitation period is identified. In litigation matters where the client was a minor or under a disability then the primary and longstop limitation periods might not apply and a longer destruction date will be needed. Where the work is 'relevant business' under the Money Laundering Regulations 2003 (MLR) it will be necessary to store a record of the transaction for five years after its completion, supporting the usual six-year period employed by most firms on most matters.

In most practices archiving or file storage is the poor relation of support functions. It is not given the attention or the investment that it deserves, and tends to be treated as a necessary evil. Elevating its status and attending properly to it would mean that:

- little or no fee earner time is wasted in trying to locate archived files;
- deeds and other documents are stored safely as a service to the client;
- there will potentially be evidence to refute any claim that may be forthcoming at some date in the future;
- expensive space is not used for storing files that otherwise might be archived or destroyed.

The momentum must be maintained throughout the life of the file, from inception, to file opening, undertaking the work, closing the file and archiving. Unfortunately, archiving the file tends to be very low on any fee earner's agenda. This in turn means that files that should be archived remain in the fee earner's room taking up unnecessary space and resulting in an untidy work environment. Ad hoc filing such as this may also present health and safety hazards in the office with passageways and fire exits being obstructed. The longer those files are left, the less the inclination to deal with them. This also makes it more likely that many of the problems that were identified in the file closure procedure could arise.

Prompt archiving should always be encouraged but not to the point of being unduly precipitous in so doing. The costs of withdrawing a file from storage if a minor query arises shortly after completion of the matter should be considered, especially where commercial archivist services are used. The fee earner should submit a request for authorisation to close the file to the accounts department, which may then check whether there are any outstanding issues that need to be addressed (balances on ledgers, any unpaid invoices). If not, an authorisation form is signed and returned to the fee earner.

The fee earner then prepares the file for archiving. This should involve thinning the file out by removing redundant drafts and paperwork. Consideration should be given as to whether or not it is necessary to keep copies of e-mails, faxes and original correspondence relating to the same matter. This is in effect storing matters in triplicate. It will take time to check through the file, but it is necessary.

Archiving is an expensive process whether the storage is on site or off. Space costs money. If every file is reduced by about one-third in size, this will have a considerable impact on the area needed for storage and the ancillary costs. When checking the file the fee earner needs to ensure that only the relevant papers for storage are in the file. Original deeds, wills, and personal items from the client on loan, such as marriage certificates and other official documents should be returned, with a receipt requested. If the client wants such documents to be stored by the practice they must be stored separately since they will be destroyed with the file if left on it. This can cause considerable problems and may result in a claim.

EXAMPLE   **Destruction of unregistered title deeds**

The firm had been instructed in the purchase of a property on behalf of the client some years ago. It was an unregistered title, and remained so after completion. Many years later the client approached the firm to sell the property. He produced a letter from the firm to say that they were keeping the deeds in safe custody. An exhaustive search was carried out. There was no trace in the deeds register of the title deeds. It became apparent that the deeds had been left on the file, which had been destroyed. The property was liable to first registration on sale. The sale was lost, the client withdrew instructions. A substantial claim followed, as the value of the property was adversely effected in that only a possessory title was available.

When it has been properly thinned out, the file should then be ready for archiving. They are various systems available for archiving, ranging from manual record systems to IT-based systems, to the scanning of files. The important point is that the system works effectively for the practice. However, the larger the practice the more challenging a manual system will be to ensure accuracy, and accuracy is essential if file recovery requests are to be handled smoothly and efficiently in the future.

Requests for files from storage should also follow a defined procedure. The request should be signed by a fee earner, as it is the fee earner who will be responsible for the file while it is out of the archiving system. It is not fair to expect a secretary to assume this responsibility. It is the fee earner who will be working on the file and it is the fee earner who should therefore be responsible for it. A common problem arising at this stage is that the fee earner passes on the file to someone else in the firm to deal with and no record of this is made. That fee earner may leave or forget what happened and so when attempts are made to locate the file at a later date, it cannot be traced. Any subsequent search, as well as being un-necessarily incurred will also cost money in terms of resources and time to locate the file. Such situations can cause considerable amounts of wasted time and embarrassment for the firm, as happened at a commercial practice some time ago when it was unable for a while to locate the deeds for the head office of a major bank.

Storage of clients' deeds and documents

Many practices provide a service whereby deeds, documents and valu-ables are stored on behalf of clients. Clients are invariably keen to avail themselves of this facility as it is usually free, unlike the facilities at pro-fessional storage operators and banks, which will tend to make a charge. With the storage of such items comes considerable responsibility and risks. The loss of a set of deeds or a will creates the obvious danger of the firm being sued. Storing deeds takes up space and resources, both of which have costs implications. Recognising the extent of storage costs, an increasing number of firms are raising a charge for storage. However, some are reluctant to do so because of a fear that if the practice charged for such a service, the client would go elsewhere. This has to be consid-ered against the likelihood of the client instructing the practice when the time comes, for example to sell their property or to administer an estate. It is more likely that the client will make a decision at that time based on fees rather than if the practice has provided a free storage facility. The practice needs to undertake a cost–benefit analysis to ascertain the real benefits of providing free storage to a client. A compromise is to reserve the right to charge a retrieval fee if the papers are taken elsewhere, as on a probate.

A deeds register must be kept. The register should identify the name of the client, the deed or document stored and the date placed into storage. If the document is requested and removed from storage, the name of the person it has been sent to should be noted on the register together with the date it was sent and if possible the reason it had been requested. The register might be manual or IT based. In both cases it is very important that a record of all deeds transactions is kept and not destroyed. This will provide evidence at a later date should confusion arise as to the whereabouts of the documents. Deeds need to be filed centrally, and not in safes in various locations around the office or offices, with each department operating their own deeds storage procedures. This practice tends only to lead to confusion.

It is recommended that practices do not store valuables on behalf of clients and many firms go to great lengths to avoid doing so. There are organisations better qualified than a law practice to do this, such as safety deposit box companies. If the practice is insistent on doing this then a schedule of the valuables must be drawn up and agreed with the client, who should countersign the schedule by way of agreement. Values should also be agreed, and if possible photographs taken of the items, which can be referred to in the event of theft.

The practice should also check its contents insurance policy to make sure that there is sufficient cover in case of theft or loss through an insured risk such as fire. There must also be clear instructions with the valuables as to who is entitled to collect them, as obviously ownership (or the right to production) of such items is very important just as it is with deeds and files.

The Guide provides very useful advice as to ownership and storage of documents. In particular it gives detailed guidance in Annex 12A as to which documents a solicitor is entitled to retain on termination of the retainer and what must be handed over to the client. This is particularly relevant where the practice is confronted by a request from a disgruntled client for his or her file in readiness for taking further action against the practice by way of a complaint or a claim.

Closing the file in an ordered structured manner and then storing it is very important. Storing deeds and other legal documents on behalf of a client is a professional service. Losing the file or documents may well give rise to an investigation by the Law Society's Consumer Complaints Service on the basis of inadequate professional services. Further, it might give rise to a claim for negligence.

EXAMPLE   **Loss of a will**

The firm had acted for C for many years and had prepared a will on his behalf which had been signed and then placed in the firm's strong room for safe-keeping. When C died the next of kin approached the firm and requested the will, which unfortunately could not be located. The file was gone, the drafts were gone and the will had gone. There was no choice but to proceed to administer the estate in accordance with the rules of intestacy. Shortly after distribution had taken place, the will was located in a fee earner's room. The beneficiaries under the intestacy were not the same people as the intended beneficiaries under the will. Understandably, a claim swiftly followed.

11

Money laundering

- Definitions and liability
- The substantive offences
- Secondary offences
- Privilege
- Disclosures and consents
- Tipping off
- Money Laundering Regulations 2003

Money laundering represents a significant and relatively new risk for legal practitioners. The combined effect of the Proceeds of Crime Act 2002 (POCA) and the Money Laundering Regulations 2003 (MLR) has been to make the topic a daily concern in most firms, even if only in the need to conduct identification checks on clients. The risks of non-compliance in relation to both POCA and the MLR are criminal penalties. What greater risk could advisers face than a conviction in the criminal courts accompanied by imprisonment and/or a fine? Money laundering compliance quite clearly needs to form an integral part of any firm's overall risk management strategy.

The most significant element of the money laundering regime for professional advisers is the need to make disclosures in certain circumstances on clients, opponents and others. In some places there is a duty to make such reports and in others advisers will need to do so to gain a defence to the main offences in the law. Either way, this is clearly at odds with our traditional understanding of the duty of confidentiality. In addition, the MLR impose certain regulatory responsibilities on most firms in areas such as client vetting and record keeping. Both elements of the money laundering provisions are in response to the Second EU Directive (2001/97/EC) on countering money laundering. A third Directive is now being proposed and it seems that further developments in this contentious area are merely a matter of time.

Formerly, the duty to report on clients and others was limited to situations involving drug trafficking or terrorism. POCA imposes blanket provisions in relation to any 'criminal conduct' where 'criminal property' results. Quite clearly the definitions are sufficiently wide to cover tax evasion – a particular problem in family law and much commercial work.

The situation with regard to the MLR is complicated by the fact that they are not stated to apply to all law firms – merely to certain activities that may or may not occur within any given practice. If the MLR do apply the firm – or the relevant parts of it – will be part of the 'regulated sector' under POCA. Taxation advice is covered as is any involvement in a 'financial or real property transaction'. It would therefore seem that most non-contentious work will be covered but that certain areas of litigation are exempt. The MLR were finally introduced for the professions, after multiple postponements, on 1 March 2004.

Definitions and liability

The definitions in relation to the main money laundering offences appear in s.340 of POCA. 'Criminal conduct' is stated to be any conduct which is illegal in the UK or would be if it were to be committed here. One of the more comical examples to emerge in this area is of a bullfighter seeking to purchase a property in the UK. Although the bullfighter might have earned their money legally while abroad, bullfighting is an offence here so the money laundering provisions would apply. At the time of going to press some fairly technical changes to the wording of POCA are being proposed in the Serious Organised Crime and Police Bill. Clause 94 of that Bill would remove the need to report instances of behaviour that is lawful where and when it occurs. Where there is an offence abroad, matters would, however, remain reportable – a good example being tax evasion revealed by the client but in another jurisdiction.

'Criminal property' is any money that represents the benefit of any person – not necessarily the client – from criminal conduct, or it could represent it in whole or in part. If, for example, a conveyancer feels that a purchase is being made wholly or in part with criminal funds then money laundering will become an issue. POCA would cover a purchase for a client who has been given money by a relative or associate if that money is believed to be criminal in its origin. There is, however, a mental element. The 'alleged offender' (adviser or client) must know or suspect that it represents such a benefit. Unlike other non-reporting offences in POCA, therefore, criminal liability should not arise from mere negligence or oversight on the part of the adviser. It remains to be seen, however, how far some element of reasonableness might develop in assessing the accused's state of mind. Under this approach the fact that the accused did not actually suspect anything untoward might not be a defence. The problem is that the wisdom of hindsight can be tough test for those accused of offences, as various advisers prosecuted for the analogous area of mortgage fraud have discovered. The authorities or prosecution may well ask the question 'Surely this must have been obvious to you?' to which the answer is 'Now you point it out to me – yes – but it was not at the time'.

Traditionally there have been three stages to money laundering. The first stage, 'placing', involves getting cash from criminal activities into the banking system. Obviously banks and building societies are more at risk here, but an increasing number of firms are experiencing clients who pay cash directly into a client account. Suspicions are all the greater when the client pays large sums of cash into the same client account at different branches on the same day or within a very short period of time. An important consideration is therefore whether the accounts department would know about such deposits and whether it would be apparent that the deposit was cash rather than cheque or draft.

The more everyday concern is the client who offers to make payments to the firm in cash in the office. Many firms have imposed an office-wide cash limit to lessen these risks – sometimes linked to concerns for staff security in relation to banking activities. As to the appropriate cash limit, it is important to note that there are no *de minimis* provisions in the law; in the words of Dame Butler-Sloss, 'an illegally obtained sum of £10 is no less susceptible to the definition of criminal property than a sum of £1m' (*P* v. *P* [2003] EWHC 2260, Fam Div, para.56).

Notwithstanding widespread calls for some common sense limits to be put on the amounts of money that should be involved when disclosure is required, proposals in the Serious Crime and Police Bill for 'threshold amounts' are limited to deposit-taking bodies and so would not unfortunately apply to legal advisers. In most cases there may be little to trigger suspicions if most clients hand over a few hundreds of pounds to ensure that the firm is in funds. There could, however, be circumstances that make a more modest amount of cash suspicious. If a client has recently completed an unsuccessful legal aid application and has declared him or herself to have nil capital, but then offers several hundreds of pounds on account of costs as a private paying client, money laundering issues could arise. The suspicion would be that a fraud had been made in the legal aid application. Wherever there are unusual circumstances in relation to cash receipts, it should be required practice to note carefully the enquiries that were made and any replies given.

In most cases, solicitors' firms will be more at risk from the later stages of 'layering' and 'integration'. Layering is where the original source of funds is obscured, for example through an investment into an apparently legitimate tenanted property. Integration occurs where the new funds are recycled with an apparently clean origin – the rental income from the property is invested in a legitimate business.

It is important to stress that money laundering liability could also arise through passive 'possession' under the offence of acquisition, use and possession (POCA, s.329). The point needs to be emphasised in partner and staff training that liability can arise as soon as a person realises or develops suspicions that funds in their client account are criminal property; funds do not actually need to move for money laundering liability to be a possibility.

The substantive offences

Liability under POCA relies on the definitions of criminal conduct and criminal property. Money laundering is then defined by s.340 as an act which 'constitutes an offence under section 327, 328 or 329' (s.340(11)(a)). The same section goes on to state that the inchoate offences of attempt, conspiracy and incitement are also covered, as is aiding and abetting one of these offences. As we will see, the deliberately wide definition given to money laundering needs to be taken into account by the money laundering reporting officer (MLRO) in situations such as attempted mortgage fraud.

The first of the three 'principal' offences is that of 'concealing' (POCA, s.327). Potentially this is an extremely wide offence since it could rely on inactivity as much as on any positive act. The section expands on the concept of concealing as being any disguising, converting, transferring or removing property from the UK. Section 327(3) explains it as concealing or 'disguising [the] nature, source, location, disposition, movement or ownership or any rights with respect to' criminal property. An example would be allowing a client to deposit funds in the client account knowing that a cheque from the firm will raise fewer questions at the bank.

Section 328 covers any arrangement that a person enters into or becomes concerned in, which (s)he 'knows or suspects facilitates (by whatever means) the acquisition, retention, use or control of criminal property by or on behalf of another person'. There is a very similar offence under s.18 of the Terrorism Act 2000, not surprisingly in relation to terrorist activities.

Finally, s.329 deals with the 'acquisition, use and possession' of criminal property. There will be considerable overlap between all the principal offences – the above example of allowing funds to pass through the client account could potentially constitute any of the three offences.

Defences

The main defence to all the principal offences is one of having made an 'authorised disclosure'. This is explained at s.338 and in most practices will be a 'disclosure which . . . is made in the course of the alleged offender's employment and in accordance with the procedure established by the employer for the purpose' (POCA s.338(5)). A similar defence appears at s.21A of the Terrorism Act in relation to the similar offences under that legislation. This means that, in effect, all personnel cover themselves by reporting suspicions internally in accordance with the firm's procedures. The buck then passes to the MLRO, who will have to decide if a report on to the authorities is needed and appropriate. There is only legal compulsion to appoint an MLRO where the MLR apply. An appointment should be made in all firms, however, as advisers in particular will need to make disclosures in certain circumstances, especially where they wish to continue to act notwithstanding the receipt of instructions that give rise to a suspicion at least of criminal property resulting from criminal conduct.

In addition to the authorised disclosure defence there is a defence of 'adequate consideration' in relation to s.329 only. Where a business provides its services for 'adequate consideration' it will have a defence. This would mean that a firm providing its usual services for a reasonable fee (for example in representing a client in confiscation proceedings under POCA) would be exempt from a charge that it has been paid with 'criminal' funds and is therefore liable itself under POCA by receiving 'criminal property' into its office account. The principal offences of concealing; arrangement; and acquisition, use and possession carry maximum sentences of 14 years' imprisonment and/or a fine.

Secondary offences

There are also two groups of secondary offences, the first of which are what might be termed the 'non-disclosure' offences. The offence of 'failure to disclose' (POCA, s.330) arises for any person who is covered by the provisions of the MLR. This provides that a person in the regulated sector commits an offence if he or she knows or suspects, or has reasonable grounds to know or suspect, that another person is engaged in money laundering and does not report this fact as soon as practicable. It is worth stressing that a reasonable suspicion test specifically applies in relation to this offence. The adviser who did not actually suspect anything untoward might still find him or herself under threat of conviction if it is felt that they should have been suspicious. Turning the proverbial 'blind eye' will not avoid liability under this provision. Again, it could yet prove that the 'hindsight test' could work very unfairly against an individual who simply did not have the time to investigate instructions as thoroughly as they should have done at the time. There is a similar provision for failure to report that applies specifically to the MLRO, which can be found in POCA, s.331.

There is a further, important condition for liability under this offence that the knowledge or suspicion 'came to him in the course of a business in the regulated sector' (POCA, s.330(3)). Without judicial guidance on this point it is difficult to know quite what this might mean. Suppose, for example, a plumber provides services for a solicitor or a member of the firm's staff at home and the plumber suggests that cash would be preferable in order to avoid paying VAT. Here the duty to make a report would not arise since the knowledge of an attempted instance of money laundering (incitement to commit an offence in itself being caught by the definition) did not arise 'in the course of a business in the regulated sector'. If, however, that plumber were a client the position would not be clear. Likewise, if a comment is made to an adviser at a social function about a client it would be difficult to know if the knowledge or suspicion that arose would be 'in the course of a business in the regulated sector' – the Law Society guidance might be taken to suggest that it possibly would (para.4.31 of the Law Society Money Laundering Guidance, at Annex 3B of the Guide (the ML Guidance)).

Defences

The main defence to a charge under s.330 is that a 'required disclosure' has been made under the firm's reporting procedures, as for the principal offences. There is also a defence that a person working in the regulated sector has not been provided with training as required by the MLR as long as they did not know or suspect the money laundering. Finally, 'legal professional privilege' is a defence for a 'professional legal adviser' under s.330(6). The actual wording of the defence is important – non-disclosure is permissible when the knowledge or suspicion comes to the adviser 'in privileged circumstances'. This wording seems specifically to invoke the area of the law of evidence known as 'legal professional privilege'.

Privilege

The issue of privilege is the most complex aspect of the law on money laundering, which is unfortunate as avoidance of liability may depend on getting it right. Very simply, privilege is not nearly so extensive as the general duty of confidentiality that all firms owe to all clients and which can only be relaxed with clear client consent or in certain exceptional circumstances (see the Guide, Principle 16.02). Privilege is the client's right to have confidential communications immune from disclosure. Where it arises, legal professional privilege protects certain communications between client and adviser from being disclosed, even in a court of law. There are two forms of privilege:

1. 'Advice privilege' – in connection with the giving of legal advice to the client; this is defined in the ML Guidance as:

    > communications between a lawyer (acting in his capacity as a lawyer) and a client ... if they are confidential and for the purpose of seeking legal advice from a lawyer or providing legal advice to a client.

2. 'Litigation privilege' – in connection with or in contemplation of legal proceedings; defined in the ML Guidance as

> Confidential communications made, after litigation has started or is 'reasonably in prospect' between a lawyer and a client, a lawyer and an agent (whether or not that agent is a lawyer) or a lawyer and a third party, for the sole and dominant purpose of litigation, whether for seeking or giving advice in relation to it, or for obtaining evidence to be used in it, or for obtaining information leading to obtaining such evidence.
>
> ML Guidance, para.4.10

Only practising lawyers can claim the benefit of legal professional privilege – the one exception being that the advice of other advisers such as accountants would be covered by this defence if they were preparing a report in litigation for an instructing practice. Given the difficulties of providing a professional service to clients without the benefit of privilege an application was mounted in 2004 for the rules to be extended to accountants also in their client activities (see 'Privilege battle defused', [2004] *Gazette*, 16 September 3).

The leading authority on advice privilege is *Three Rivers District Council* v. *Bank of England (Disclosure) (No.1)* [2003] 3 WLR 667. In a dispute concerning the collapse of BCCI the Court of Appeal held that legal advice privilege could only apply to documents passing between a client and his or her legal advisers and evidence of such communications. This decision initially defined advice privilege in much narrower terms than earlier decisions such as *Balabel* v. *Air India* [1988] Ch 317. This had provided that privilege on the 'giving of legal advice' should have a wider interpretation on 'legal advice' than might be argued. Privilege should extend beyond strict legal advice to what should prudently be done or not done in the relevant legal context – i.e. the appropriateness of proposed action. The House of Lords decision in the *Three Rivers* case seems largely to restore this wider view.

The rule that has caused some of the most complex deliberations is the rule that legal professional privilege does not apply to communications if there is a criminal or fraudulent intent behind them. This common law rule is confirmed in statute by the Police and Criminal Evidence Act 1984 (s.10(2)). This is subject to some of the most technical guidance in the ML Guidance. The suggestion is that legal professional privilege breaks down where there is a criminal or fraudulent purpose on the part of anyone seeking that advice but that the adviser needs to realise that this is the case to be culpable (see ML Guidance, especially paras 4.12–4.14 and 4.37–4.40). In practice, few MLROs are likely to take the risk of incurring liability from such complex provisions, and statistics from the National Criminal Intelligence Service (NCIS) in 2004 suggest that 'defensive' reporting has become commonplace.

Curiously the MLRO does not have the defence of privilege to non-disclosure under POCA, s.331. This could be taken to mean that if the MLRO receives an internal report from an adviser where it is clear that privilege did apply, he or she is under a duty in any event to make a disclosure to protect themselves. This much was suggested to the Solicitors Family Law Association in an opinion that they commissioned soon after POCA took effect (advice by Roy Amlot QC). The view of the Law Society, however, is that the MLRO would have a defence of 'reasonable excuse' to not reporting under s.331(6), which does seem more appropriate (see the ML Guidance, para.4.36). Whether this would actually be the case again remains to be seen in a prosecution on the point, failing which it is to be hoped that the ML Guidance is accepted by the Treasury, in which case it would be a defence for a person to show that they were acting in good faith and in pursuance of this Guidance.

One further area of concern is that privilege is not a defence to a charge under the principal offences found in POCA, ss.327–329, so the anomaly could arise whereby an adviser could have a defence to a charge under s.330 for failure to report but could still face prosecution under s.327 for 'concealing' their suspicions. This means that a criminal lawyer could be convicted for not disclosing his or her instructions to the authorities even though any common-sense understanding of privilege would suggest that it would need to apply in such circumstances. The Law Society recognises this nonsensical possibility but comments that an action would be 'unlikely' in such circumstances (see the ML Guidance, para.4.52). The fact that it is even a possibility suggests that there was an oversight in drafting the law – the whole area of privilege having been written into the Second EU Directive at a late stage under the protests of various Bar associations. It is bound to be a matter of concern that such important provisions in relation to the administration of justice and the potential liability of its practitioners carry such doubts about their application.

Disclosures and consents

When a report is made the firm is placed in a difficult position with its client. Generally the law prohibits any intimation that a disclosure has been made, but equally the firm risks liability under the principal offences – most obviously an arrangement under POCA, s.328 – if it continues to act. Having made a disclosure the firm needs 'appropriate consent' to continue to act. This could be actual consent or, in an attempt to keep any waiting period to reasonable proportions, the firm is deemed to have consent if it waits for seven working days and does not hear that consent is refused.

If, during the seven working days, NCIS indicates that consent is refused the 'moratorium' period commences. NCIS then has 31 days (not working days) to gain an order. If it does not do so the firm may continue to act and will have a defence to charges under the principal offences if it does.

An MLRO who consents to the firm continuing to act for a client after a disclosure has been made but before consent is received or these periods expire takes the risk of prosecution under POCA, s.336. Some extremely difficult situations could arise. Suppose that NCIS will not reply and a firm has exchanged contracts in a conveyancing transaction with a completion due before the consent is received or the moratorium period expires. The rather unedifying choice would be between the risk of civil liability for failure to complete on the one hand (and so having to field some fairly blunt questions from the client) and possible criminal liability under POCA on the other. The hope would be that such situations do not arise, but there remain concerns about the resources available to NCIS and it is a possibility. Rather disturbingly, one firm has recounted the experience of requesting urgent permission to complete a conveyancing transaction the next day only to be told that it would have to decide for itself whether it could do so. This may become more commonplace experience as the number of 'defensive' disclosures continues to increase, unless the resources within NCIS are increased.

Tipping off

There is a third group of offences beyond the principal offences and the reporting offences, which concern notifying any person about a disclosure. The best known of these offences is 'tipping off' (POCA, s.333). This offence is committed where a report has already been made and a disclosure is made that is likely to prejudice an investigation. There is a similar offence under POCA, s.342 – 'prejudicing an investigation'. This arises where a person knows or suspects that an appropriate officer (e.g. customs officer, police officer) is acting or is proposing to act in connection with an investigation and makes a disclosure.

There are two widespread concerns in the profession about possible tipping off liability. The first is that in failing to act where the firm should obviously be so doing the firm may, in effect, be 'tipping off' the client about a disclosure – failure to complete a conveyancing transaction on the due date, for example. Since s.336 makes no provision for the MLRO to provide consent where he or she feels that this is a risk, it has to be assumed that Parliament did not consider this to be a risk, unless drafting error is again in evidence. The more pressing problem for a firm caught up in this situation is what the firm can tell the client. The conclusion of many firms is that it is necessary to lie to the client – the file is missing, the fee earner is not available or there is a problem elsewhere. For professional advisers subject to the duties of good faith towards clients to be reduced to such a conclusion is highly unsatisfactory. True, there is a defence to any professional charges arising from disclosures (see POCA, s.339(4)) but that is hardly the point. This situation is one to consider carefully in relation to secretaries. If the adviser is trying to avoid discussions with an irate client, the secretary might come under increased pressure to 'get the file and tell me what's going on'. This very real possibility suggests that secretaries and administrators should be included in the money laundering training that the firm should or has to provide.

The other concern that many practitioners have expressed is the extent of information about money laundering law and the duty to make disclosures that the firm can share with the client. This led to some concerned contributions to the correspondence columns of the Law Society's *Gazette* in early 2004 (see, for example, 'Hard earned trust' [2004] *Gazette*, 1 April). The risks are not so great as many fear, since s.333 provides:

> A person commits an offence if –
>
> (a) he knows or suspects that a disclosure falling within section 337 or 338 *has been made*, and
> (b) he makes a disclosure which is likely to prejudice any investigation which might be conducted following the disclosure referred to in paragraph (a) [emphasis added].

The wording of the offence makes it clear that liability under this offence only arises where the disclosure has already been made. Caution is needed in a couple of respects, however. First, the point at which a disclosure 'has been made' under the definition in POCA, s.338(5) is when it is reported internally to the MLRO and not externally to NCIS. Second, there is still potential liability before that point under an inchoate version of one of the principal offences. This would mean that an adviser unwise enough to explain to a client how he or she could avoid another firm reporting to NCIS about them could be charged with a conspiracy, attempt or incitement to commit one of the principal offences or of aiding and abetting another person to commit one of the offences (see the definition of money laundering at POCA, ss.340(11)(b) and (c)).

The net effect is that it is difficult to see how a firm could be seen to have committed either the offence of tipping off or the offence of prejudicing an investigation by including a clear warning in its terms of business or equivalent correspondence. Many take the view that it is appropriate to warn clients of the duty to disclose out of fairness to them, and it is becoming increasingly accepted practice. Whether the warning is included in standard terms of business or actual correspondence to the client is a matter of style.

Defence: privilege

There is one instance of seemingly blatant tipping off that is sanctioned by the ML Guidance. The view of the Law Society is that:

if a client is aware that his bank has been in contact with the police, he is entitled to seek advice on his legal position and his legal adviser is entitled to
advise him that he may be the subject of a money laundering investigation
without the risk of being prosecuted for either offence, even if as a result such
advice might prejudice the investigation.

ML Guidance, para.4.74

Clearly, any fee earner finding themselves in this situation would be well
advised to proceed with great care. The justification for the Law Society's
advice on this point seems to be legal professional privilege, which is stated
to be a defence to both of these charges but only where there is no 'criminal purpose'. If the Law Society is right and the client should be entitled to
this advice the adviser would have to ensure that his or her advice fell short
of what might be argued to be 'aiding and abetting' one of the principal
offences. The advice would need to be confined to the specific situation of
the client and not extend to the steps needed to escape liability other than
the proper steps of making a voluntary disclosure in relation to any money
laundering charge.

It should be noted that the standard of privilege in relation to these
two offences is not the same as under the duty to disclose in POCA, s.330.
Whereas the defence to non-disclosure under s.330(6) talks about the
information coming to the adviser 'in privileged circumstances' the
equivalent wording in ss.333(3) and 342(4) (identical in both sections) is
that the lawyer is protected if a disclosure is:

(a) to (or to a representative of) a client of the professional legal adviser in
connection with the giving by the legal adviser of legal advice to the
client, or
(b) to any person in connection with legal proceedings or contemplated
legal proceedings.

This wording seems to invoke the concepts of advice and litigation privilege but may be wider. Both sections, however, remove the defence
where there is a 'criminal purpose' (ss.333(4) and 342(5)). This led NCIS
to argue that the legal adviser could, in effect, never reveal a disclosure
under this privilege defence since there would always be a 'criminal
purpose' on somebody's part. This was to be one of the main issues in the
case of *P* v. *P* [2003] EWHC 2260, Fam Div.

EXAMPLE   *P* v. *P*

This was a divorce case with substantial assets involved – some £19 million.
W filed for divorce in 2002 and, at a conference in June 2003 to consider
replies to questions put to H's accountants, W's solicitors became concerned

that they might be committing an offence under POCA, s.328, in that they formed the view that the source of H's funds were suspect and the settlement under discussion could therefore be an 'arrangement'. They therefore sought to protect themselves by making a report to NCIS on 18 June and gaining consent to continue to act.

NCIS had been asked for a reply within seven days and were also asked if W's solicitors could report the disclosure to their client. No written reply was received, and in telephone calls they received incorrect advice from NCIS that:

- no report was needed unless money was about to change hands; and
- if the money was not passing through the solicitors' hands no report was needed in any event.

The NCIS officer also said that the client could not be advised of the report or it would amount to tipping off under POCA, s.333.

W's solicitors felt that they were in an impossible situation from this advice and applied ex parte for a ruling on their situation. A number of interested parties were joined into the eventual hearing: the Law Society, the Bar Council, Inland Revenue and NCIS. H's solicitors learned of what was happening by obtaining a copy of the court records on why the ex parte application had been adjourned and also applied to be party to the hearing.

In relation to privilege under s.333 (tipping off), s.342 (prejudicing an investigation) and the general duty to disclose in s.330, NCIS questioned whether there could ever be circumstances where a report was justified as it would always 'further a criminal purpose' on somebody's part.

W's solicitors could have continued to act after the expiry of the seven-day period from the date of their letter but sought a ruling to clarify their position. H's solicitors had not made a disclosure since they did not consider on the basis of their instructions that they needed to do so.

It was held that:

- liability for an 'arrangement' under s.328 could arise well before the point of execution of the arrangement in question; but
- there is nothing in s.328 to prevent an adviser from taking instructions from a client. If the adviser then forms a suspicion that they or the client might become involved in an arrangement an authorised disclosure should be made;
- there is a duty in ancillary proceedings on legal advisers of full and frank disclosure to the client (*Clibbery* v. *Allan* [2002] Fam 261), and: 'In general terms the professional duties in family proceedings do, in my view, appear to attract the protection of section 333(3) and 342(4) in order to permit a legal adviser to inform, for instance, the other side that a disclosure either will be or has been made to the NCIS' (para.60);

- having complied with the duty to report under s.328 'there is nothing in the statute to require a solicitor to delay in informing his client. Either he is entitled to do so forthwith . . . or he is not entitled to do so at all. There is no middle ground' (para.66). Nonetheless, good practice might be to allow the authorities their seven working days to conduct their investigations, but this was not obligatory;
- there is no need to make repeated disclosures on the same circumstances (para.69).

The effect of this decision has been much debated. Technically, the decision is not binding in any criminal proceedings under POCA since it is a civil case, but it would be a harsh conviction indeed if an adviser found themselves under prosecution and had been following the guidelines that emerge from this case. The judgment was helpful in clarifying the approach of the divorce lawyer taking instructions on the financial position of the parties and the following line of logic seems to be broadly acceptable to the Law Society (see [2004] *Gazette*, 15 January), the Solicitors Family Law Association (SFLA) and the Bar Council in its advice to counsel.

1. The adviser can safely take instructions without fear that in so doing they are entering an 'arrangement' contrary to s.328.
2. If no reasonable suspicion arises of money laundering the SFLA recommends a letter to the client advising them of the future possibility of a report if circumstances change.
3. Where at least a reasonable suspicion arises in such circumstances, an authorised disclosure might be necessary to gain a defence to possible charges under POCA, ss.327–329 – so a disclosure would need to be made to the MLRO or the sole practitioner will need to report to NCIS.
4. Given that a disclosure would have to be made to gain a defence of authorised disclosure to the principal offences – so that the adviser is able to continue to act – the issue of whether the adviser in person would be obliged to disclose under their firm's procedures under s.330 (duty to disclose) would seem to be irrelevant.
5. Family lawyers will sometimes want to discuss the need for a disclosure with their client. The practice of so doing was sanctioned by the Law Society in its guidance for family lawyers ([2004] *Gazette*, 15 January). Whether the client agrees to a voluntary disclosure with the adviser or not they will need clear advice on the implications of the regime and their potential liability.
6. If the making of a report is not discussed with the client, can the client later be informed? The SFLA advises that it will 'depend on the facts of the case', but as long as the adviser has no intention of furthering a criminal purpose in making a disclosure to the client

they seem likely to have a defence to either of the disclosure offences (ss.333 and 342) if they tell the client what they have done. It should be borne in mind that just because an adviser *may* inform the client of a report it does not mean that they *must* do so (see the ML Guidance, para.4.71).

7. If the adviser withdraws from acting at that stage the firm would not have to disclose under s.330 if privilege applied. A report would seem to be necessary where the information came from the opponent since communication between parties cannot be privileged.

8. If the adviser is to continue to act where there is at least a reasonable suspicion of money laundering the 'appropriate consent' of NCIS is needed as set out in POCA, s.335. This may afford a defence to the principal offences but there may be difficult situations where the adviser feels that they wish to withdraw anyway on professional grounds.

Many firms have come to the conclusion that the situation outside family law is different, as advisers are not subject to the same duty of openness. It may theoretically be the case that the adviser could inform the client that they have made a disclosure on them but why, in most instances, would they wish to do so? In non-litigation areas it is more likely that legal professional privilege would not extend to the information that has led to the knowledge or suspicion of money laundering in any event, so a disclosure will be necessary to avoid liability for non-disclosure under s.330.

It might be tempting to adopt a policy of disclosing anything, on grounds that this is the safest course of action for the firm. Care would be needed with this approach. The protection under s.339(4) against professional liability does not extend to contractual issues and the duty of confidentiality is an implied term of the solicitor–client retainer. It would follow that if a client could show that their firm had made a disclosure on them where there were no reasonable grounds to do so the client might have a claim against the firm.

Money Laundering Regulations 2003

Before the MLR took effect on 1 March 2004 solicitors' firms were only subject to earlier regulations if they provided advice in the area of financial services. Since the government wanted to bring into the regulatory framework all relevant activities whoever was offering them it chose to implement the provisions of the Second EU Directive by reference to activities rather than designated professional groups. The net result is far from clear: although accountants in private practice are clearly caught by the MLR whatever their practice area, solicitors are not. A firm, or particular part of it, is only covered if it is covered by one of the following areas.

(2) For the purposes of these Regulations, 'relevant business' means –

[. . .]

(i) the provision by way of business of advice about the tax affairs of another person by a body corporate or unincorporate or, in the case of a sole practitioner, by an individual;

[. . .]

(l) the provision by way of business of legal services by a body corporate or unincorporate or, in the case of a sole practitioner, by an individual and which involves participation in a financial or real property transaction (whether by assisting in the planning or execution of any such transaction or otherwise by acting for, or on behalf of, a client in any such transaction);

(m) the provision by way of business of services in relation to the formation, operation or management of a company or a trust . . .

MLR, reg.1(2)

Being caught by the provisions on 'relevant business' means that the firm, or the relevant part of it, is in the 'regulated sector'. Doubts remain about which areas of law are in or out of the 'regulated sector'. The ML Guidance falls short of exempting areas, but suggests that the following 'would not generally be viewed as "participation in financial transactions"' (para.3.12):

- payment on account of costs or payment of a bill;
- legal advice;
- participation in litigation;
- will writing;
- publicly funded work.

Even this advice has to be read with some care. It may be true, for example, that will writing is not a financial transaction as such, but it often involves advice on taxation and so presumably could be covered on those grounds. There have been similar arguments on ancillary proceedings in family law work – should they be seen as being merely 'participation in litigation' or, when advice is given on the transfer of equity in the matrimonial home or the possible suitability of a 'clean break' lump sum settlement, advice on a 'financial or real property transaction'? Little wonder that most firms have taken the view that the MLR should be seen to apply to the whole firm and that any exceptions are not helpful. The Law Society seems to suggest that this may be the most appropriate approach where there is doubt, with its advice at para.3.14 of the ML Guidance to take a 'cautious approach' on the issue.

Where the MLR do apply the main requirements are that there is a need to:

- appoint a money laundering reporting officer (MLRO);
- adopt reporting and control procedures;
- train 'relevant employees';
- conduct identity checking with most clients;
- maintain certain records for future information.

If the MLR apply it is a criminal offence not to follow them, regardless of whether money laundering is actually happening in the firm. The maximum penalty for non-compliance will be two years' imprisonment and/or a fine for those concerned with management (MLR, reg.3(2)). This caused some concern to the Law Society in its response to the draft Regulations when they appeared, since the Second EU Directive did not require criminal penalties.

The best view on training is that potential liability extends to anyone within the practice. The fairest approach is therefore to include some mention of money laundering compliance in training for all personnel in the practice. For some this might be limited to the dangers of liability for tipping off and why conducting identification checks is so important, but for others it should be very much more detailed – fee earners and accounts personnel most obviously. The Law Society also recommends that training should not be seen as a one-off obligation and it should therefore be kept up to date in a 'rolling programme' (ML Guidance, para.3.20).

The main practical implication of being part of the regulated sector is that it becomes necessary to check the identification of most new clients. This gives rise to the issue in many personal injury firms as to whether they are indeed covered by the MLR. If the pattern of work is such that the firm does not meet its referred clients in person, as has become commonplace in recent years, there are very real advantages in taking the view that the work is outside the regulated sector since the difficulties of identification checking at a distance are avoided. The actual provisions on the checking required are complicated by a distinction between a 'business relationship' and a 'one-off transaction'. This distinction is based on the operations of the financial services sector and is not particularly helpful in legal practice. A 'business relationship' is defined in the MLR, reg.2 as:

> any arrangement the purpose of which is to facilitate the carrying out of transactions on a frequent, habitual or regular basis where the total amount of any payments to be made by any person to any other in the course of the arrangement is not known or capable of being ascertained at the outset.

This may be clear enough with a customer who wishes to open a bank account, but is anything but when a new client instructs the firm for the first time. Will this be the start of an ongoing client relationship or will it prove to be just a 'one-off'? Neither party would be likely at that stage to know.

The MLR actually provide that checking is needed if the firm and client form, or agree to form, a business relationship or in respect of any one-off transaction where the firm knows or suspects that the transaction involves money laundering or where a payment of 15,000 euro or more is to be made by or to the client; or (even more confusingly) in respect of two or more one-off transactions where it appears that the transactions are linked and involve, in total, the payment of 15,000 euro or more by or to the client. When checking is required it must occur 'as soon as is reasonably practicable after contact is first made'. The MLR refer to the greater risks with the client who is not met in person. There is a requirement that the firm's procedures should 'take into account the greater potential for money laundering which arises when [the client] is not physically present when being identified' (MLR, reg.4(3)(b)). Practices are well advised to insist on the production of the necessary evidence at the outset: 'where satisfactory evidence of identity is not obtained, the business relationship or one-off transaction must not proceed any further' (MRL, reg.4(3)(c)).

The MLR provide for a twofold test. The evidence produced must reasonably show that the person is who they claim to be and the person conducting the check must also personally be satisfied by the evidence produced. Firms should not act for undisclosed principals, but the standard of checking here appears to be slightly lower, though whether firms will want to make this distinction is questionable (ML Guidance, para.3.36).

The ML Guidance suggests that firms need to keep all copy evidence on file and there is a recommendation that the evidence should have noted on it the details of when the original was seen and by whom, certifying it to be a true copy. Colour copies of passport details should not be taken to avoid any possibility of it being passed off as a real passport. Sample forms and further guidelines appear in the *Lexcel Office Procedures Manual*.

The record keeping requirements are found at MLR, reg.6 which provides that a copy of the evidence must be maintained for at least five years from the end of the business relationship or the one-off transaction(s). In addition, details of all transactions (in effect, the matter file) must also be maintained for at least five years from the end of the matter. This has led most firms to conclude that some form of central record of identification evidence is essential, especially where repeat work is done for regular clients. The risk otherwise is that required evidence is destroyed with the file after the normal period of years, leaving the firm without evidence on later or longer-running matters from the same client. The alternative is that the client has to produce fresh evidence of identity and address on each occasion that the client instructs the firm and this is then maintained on every matter file.

One final observation. Compliance with money laundering legislation brings with it a considerable extra cost for legal practices. Beyond the obvious costs of management time for the MLRO and others who become involved on decisions about disclosures, there is the simple administrative cost of opening a file – a procedure that might be repeated many hundreds of times per week in some larger firms. There is scant appreciation for this burden. The threat of prosecution, however, remains a very real one for all practitioners. It is to be hoped that prosecution will prove to be the last resort and does not occur when mistakes are made. Fairness seems to suggest that prosecution should be reserved for those who knowingly involve themselves in improper activities.

12

Managing a project

- Objectives and commitment
- Responsibility
- The programme: external or internal assessment?
- The office manual
- Implementation of the programme

It is all well and good for a firm to debate what it needs to do to improve its risk profile. The partners might also agree that an application for an external quality award such as Lexcel would be beneficial. These decisions have to be put into effect, however, and someone will need to assume responsibility for the project.

The question of whether the firm should secure the services of a consultant could arise at the outset or might arise once the practice has decided what it wants to achieve and in what timescale. Either way, it is important that any adviser who is appointed should have relevant experience. A lifetime in quality control in industry will certainly equip an individual with expertise on quality management principles and the contents of standards such as ISO 9001, but this is not the same thing as knowing how quality management can be made to work in the particular environment of the legal professional partnership. The Lexcel Office of the Law Society has run consultancy training for those wishing to be recognised as practitioners in that standard for many years and maintains lists of consultants with contact details. Even if gaining recognition under that standard is not a priority, it might be advisable to approach those who have been through this training. Lexcel is designed to improve the risk profile of practices and the standard will form an excellent agenda for those who wish simply to improve their management effectiveness or risk profile. It would be as well also to ask potential advisers what experience they have of quality projects elsewhere within the legal sector and with what success. The risk of using consultants who do not have experience of the legal sector is that they will provide inappropriate advice at considerable expense. Most firms will probably be willing to share their views on the service provided by way of a short telephone reference.

Objectives and commitment

Whether in conjunction with an adviser or not, an important first step is to determine the objectives of the programme. Where Lexcel certification will not be sought the objectives could be linked to a reduction in claims or a reduction in the specific problems that have been experienced – the elimination of claims resulting from failure to pay off second charges in conveyancing being one example. It is important that the quality or risk project is not seen as an end in itself. If people within the firm are to be asked to spend time reviewing what they do and why, undertake the necessary training and then adapt their daily patterns of working, there has to be some real advantage in mind. Projects often fail where gaining the 'badge' of recognition under Lexcel or another quality mark is all that can be agreed upon. Being told by a major client that the firm needs to obtain recognition under ISO 9001 or Lexcel might direct the attention of the partners to the risk of losing that client if they fail to do so, but it is hardly likely to engender support for the programme internally. If the partnership objectives are 'to secure Lexcel recognition to keep our insurers happy' the firm is likely to struggle through the project at best. What is needed is some real commitment that suggests that the partners believe that the programme is worthwhile.

Why, then, should a firm undertake a risk or quality project? The Lexcel Office list the benefits of their standard as being:

- increased profitability;
- to minimise mistakes;
- effective risk management;
- establishing a framework to meet legislative requirements – money laundering compliance being the example provided;
- improved client care;
- provision of a competitive advantage;
- improved marketability to prospective clients;
- management efficiency;
- assistance with compliance with new practice rules – the examples given are business operations and client relation rules;
- assistance with best value provisions for local authorities.

This list is built on solid evidence from the few hundred practices to have gained recognition under Lexcel to date and should provide some useful points for any discussion on the subject at a partnership meeting.

One of the most important points to take on board at the early stages of a project is that without real support from the partners there is a risk of considerable amounts of time and expenditure being wasted. Staff will take their lead from the way that partners act. If the official line is that the firm is committed to succeeding in an application for recognition for

Lexcel, but the quite public approach taken by the partners in one department is that the project is a waste of time, these detractors may well get their way and undermine the project. This should not be seen as acceptable behaviour and there is a need for all to accept the principle of 'cabinet responsibility', whatever their personal views. Leadership by all partners and senior personnel is key and can best be evidenced by attending meetings and training and following any procedures themselves. Leadership by example is essential. The support of others should therefore be a precondition of any partner or manager taking on responsibility for the project.

Responsibility

The need for someone to lead the project is reflected in most of the quality standards. Lexcel has a provision at section 1.5 requiring: 'one designated individual who has particular responsibility for the quality system'. There is a similar provision for legal aid provision at SQM section G3.1: 'a named individual is responsible for overseeing all quality procedures used by the organisation'. ISO 9001 is slightly more demanding in that it talks about: 'Top management shall appoint a member of management who, irrespective of other responsibilities shall have responsibility and authority . . .' (5.5.2).

The issue of authority is also seen in section 1.5 of Lexcel where it states that the individual with responsibility for the system must have 'sufficient authority and seniority to raise concerns regarding the quality system and to have any such issues resolved'. Taken along with section 1.4, which talks about the written quality policy 'setting out the organisation's commitment to quality and overall policy', it is intended to confront the idea that Lexcel can be an unimportant project that has little to do with the mainstream management issues of the practice. Under Lexcel 2004 there may well therefore be potential non-compliances if a number of partners express doubts about the programme or if the same problems surface year after year. Either situation could suggest that there is insufficient commitment to the programme or that the person in charge of it lacks the will or authority to have matters resolved.

The programme: external or internal assessment?

Once the objectives have been settled and issues of responsibility and 'buy-in' at partner level have been dealt with, a programme of action will need to be established. The firm could choose to set its own objectives and then manage its own internal programme. The advantage of opening the firm up to external assessment, as through Lexcel, is that the practice is then confronted with a clear date by which things have to be in place. It is not impossible for a dynamic and committed leader of a quality or risk programme to achieve what they wish without an external assessment, but most programmes will benefit from having this clear focus. Another benefit of the external assessment is that peer pressure emerges and can be harnessed by the quality partner or manager. Nobody will want to be the person who holds up assessment and the fear of failure that is often quite pronounced in lawyers can be converted to good effect.

The office manual

The first step in any programme is to prepare a manual. Again, all the main quality standards other than Investors in People agree on the need for this manual and most impose some obligations of 'document control' – ie the need for proper authorisation in relation to changes (see ISO 9001, 4.2.2 and SQM, section G4). In Lexcel the need for an office manual is found at section 4.6, which provides that:

> Practices will maintain an office manual collating information on office practice, which must be available to all members of the practice. Practices will document their arrangements to:
> a: Note each page with the date and/or issue.
> b: Review the manual at least annually.
> c: Update the manual and record the date of amendments.

In most firms the increasing use of computer systems means that there is no longer a need to print off multiple copies of the manual as it can be contained on the firm's system or intranet. This has the obvious advantage that there is no longer a need to struggle to ensure that all holders update their copies when procedures are altered, since changes are made to the system and all personnel are encouraged always to consult the up-to-date procedures on the system. Where this is the case it is important to add word-search facilities if at all possible so that users are quickly directed to the relevant provisions. It is also a good idea to place a linking icon especially for the manual on the main front panel.

There are obvious advantages in using an off-the-shelf manual such as the *Lexcel Office Procedures Manual* but there are dangers also. The preface to that document stresses that it should be used as a precedent and not a draft, but many firms show little imagination in adapting its contents to their situation.

The first stage of the programme – drawing up the manual setting out how the firm will meet its obligations – can take several weeks or months. In many cases extra time spent on the project at this stage can prove invaluable later. If the task of preparing the manual is opened up to consultation at this stage there are likely to be fewer problems when it later comes to implementation. The partner who sits in isolation writing up procedures for the firm may well find an adverse reaction when he or she circulates it at the firm. Writing up the procedures that all will have to observe should be a team project. Human nature also means that we are more likely to accept what we think we have been consulted upon. One device that can prove highly effective is to write a general manual that applies across the firm, but then add a departmental appendix where issues of importance to that work area or variations to normal principles can be recorded. The alternative is to have too standardised a manual, which might alienate certain sections of the firm or to have multiple manuals that are insufficient in the way of core procedures. A checklist of issues that might feature in this sort of departmental appendix can be found in the *Lexcel Office Procedures Manual* at Appendix 8A.

| EXAMPLE | General provision in office manual for undertakings |

The firm determines that in order to minimise the risks of inappropriate undertakings they will all require partner consent. This would prove unworkable in the conveyancing department, however, in relation to certain routine undertakings as commonly given in relation to the discharge of mortgages. The firm records its general procedure on the point but the Conveyancing appendix provides the circumstances where fee earners in the department may provide undertakings without specific partner consent.

One of the challenges is to pitch the procedures at a level that will enhance the general level of service provided by the firm but will also be achievable. If, for example, the frequency of file reviews under section 6.6 of Lexcel is set at one file per fee earner per year, an assessor would make a finding that the procedure was not in effective operation. At the other extreme, a firm that determined to check 50 per cent of its files per month would be assessed to this standard. If it found itself having reviewed only 40 per cent of files at an assessment it would be non-compliant. An assessor seeks evidence that the firm is complying with its procedures. Where this is not the case the firm must show that it has addressed this under-performance. Alternatively, if what is happening is potentially compliant with the standard, the firm might elect to change its procedures. In the above example, therefore, the firm could apply more time to its very ambitious file review arrangements or change the procedure to require file reviews in 30 per cent of its matters per month (still way above what would be normal in most firms), in which case the assessor has already seen evidence that the firm is complying with that requirement.

Implementation of the programme

When the manual is completed there will need to be a 'start date' for the new ways of working. Some firms choose to launch the whole system on a given day while others phase the new regime in – perhaps file opening one month and then confirmation of instructions to clients the next. At a Lexcel assessment the inspector will look at files only from that start date, so there is no need to change files retrospectively to ensure compliance. All work done on continuing files after that date should be to the new system of working, however.

The most common mistake at this stage of the programme is to stint on implementation training. Manuals are to be consulted and are not always designed to make for easy reading for most. Real attempts should therefore be made to explain to all personnel what the new systems now require of them. More often than not the requirements will be to continue to do what they always should have been doing, but new procedures need special attention. It is recommended that the firm produces a 'training guide' to the quality or risk system, which can then be used on subsequent induction training programmes.

Training is simply one form of communication. It remains important in many other ways to maintain communication throughout the project. There is no reason not to be open with staff and clients on the fact that the firm is working on its programme. Staff, in particular, might be suspicious if little information is forthcoming. The Lexcel Office has launched with some success its 'commitment scheme' whereby the intention of a firm to apply for certification is recorded. This ensures that the practice is kept informed of developments in the standard. In some cases discounts have been given on indemnity insurance rates simply from this declaration of intent. There is one other compelling reason to be open to clients before an assessment: the ruling on client confidentiality is that the client's consent is needed for an assessor to inspect their files. An explanation of the issue of consent can be found in the introduction to the *Lexcel Assessment Guide* (pp.13–14) and some recommended wording for client care letters can be found in precedents in the *Lexcel Office Procedures Manual*.

When the firm undergoes an external assessment it may feel that success at that stage is the end of a difficult but important process. It is not the end of the process, however. At very least the programme will need to be maintained. The firm's experience will need to be considered and data on issues such as file reviews, claims and complaints will need to be examined to see if the programme really is achieving the benefits that had been hoped for. Principles of quality management suggest that this experience should be taken forward and that the firm should continue to develop its system. In Lexcel there is a requirement at section 1.6 that the review of the operation of the quality system must 'show the part that the quality system is intended to play in the future strategy of the practice over the next 12 months at least'. Risks that are already known about may be better controlled but they will not have gone away and new risks will continue to emerge. The firm that has embraced the principles espoused in this book will not find itself in a risk-free environment but it should be confident that it is doing what can reasonably be expected of it to minimise its exposure to problems. The insurers will regard the firm as a better proposition than others and the clients should receive a more reliable service. The partners should be free to spend more time getting on with fee earning and related management work and less time should be wasted sorting out avoidable problems. The enhanced levels of efficiency are likely to evidence themselves in increased profitability.

Index